BLACKS IN AND OUT OF THE LEFT

The W. E. B. Du Bois Lectures

BLACKS IN AND OUT OF THE LEFT

Michael C. Dawson

HARVARD UNIVERSITY PRESS
Cambridge, Massachusetts
London, England
2013

Library of Congress Cataloging-in-Publication Data
Dawson, Michael C., 1951–
    Blacks in and out of the left / Michael C. Dawson.
        p.   cm. – (The W. E. B. Du Bois lectures)
    Includes bibliographical references and index.
    ISBN 978-0-674-05768-5 (alk. paper)
    1. African Americans—Politics and government—20th century.
    2. African Americans—Politics and government—21st century.
    3. African Americans—Race identity—Political aspects. 4. Right and
    left (Political science)—History. 5. Social movements—United States—
    History. 6. Political culture—United States—History. I. Title.

    E185.615.D395   2013
    323.1196'073—dc23   2012039298

Contents

Preface   vii

1. Foundational Myths: Recovering
   and Reconciling Narratives of Resistance   1

2. Power to the People?   41

3. Who and What Killed the Left   126

4. Modern Myths: Constructing
   Visions of the Future   175

References   213
Notes   221
Acknowledgments   229
Index   233

Preface

In the fall of 2009 I was invited to deliver the W. E. B. Du Bois lectures by the Du Bois Institute at Harvard University. This book represents a substantial revision of those lectures. The original title of those lectures was "Blacks and the Left: Past, Present, and Future." But that was not quite right. In one way or another blacks and black movements in the Americas have been constituent parts of radical progressive movements since the Founding, well before anything such as a left had been conceived. African Americans, their organizations, and/or black movements had been constituent parts of pre–Revolutionary War radical actions, the antislavery and suffrage movements, and the populist and farmers' movements that swept the South and West during the last few decades of the nineteenth century. And, as Carole Horton, Jeffrey Perry, and other contemporary authors have shown, blacks had a complicated but active relationship to the growing American labor movement at the end of the 1800s. The twentieth-century relationships between African Americans and the left were arguably even more complex, and the title "Blacks and the Left" too much implied that blacks stood outside the left, either in opposition to or in alliance with it, as opposed to being a key part of the left and having a fraught relationship with its organizations and its activists.

I take the current title, *Blacks In and Out of the Left,* in at least three ways. First, the title is meant quite literally and temporally. At different times, individual African Americans and black organizations have actually been in and out of the left during specific eras and at various places, as leftist movements often had different regional and local characters during periods of heightened activism, as did the black movement itself.

Second, I also am signifying through the title that even when blacks were an active part of the left, it was common for black activism not to be a central part of activist discourses outside the black community. The same claim probably could be made even more strongly about the Asian American and Latino activism of a generation ago. In general, there was often a fairly high level of awareness among activists of color about what was going on in each other's communities, while it was often the case that white radicals of various stripes knew very little, and what they thought they knew was stupefyingly incorrect. Sociologist and former Students for a Democratic Society leader Todd Gitlin is an excellent example of someone who thinks he knew what was going on in not just nonwhite movements but also the women's as well as gay and lesbian movements. The startling lack of information he has about those movements is matched only by the vacuousness of his interpretation of that history.

Third, black radicalism and the study and analysis of it have also been in and out of scholarly discourses—mostly out, except in black studies. There are of course many scholars who have been studiously applying their talent to the study of black radicalism with excellent effect. Historians such as Mark Solomon, Robin Kelley, Carole Boyce Davies, Glenda Gilmore, Randi Storch, and Martha Biondi have greatly expanded our knowledge of race and radical movements in the United States. Philosophers such as Tommie Shelby and my colleague Robert Gooding-Williams have made important contributions analyzing radical black political thought. When we start looking at work that purports to describe the movements of the left, the origins of Marxism in the United States, or even the move to the right in the United States during the past thirty years, however, we see not only a stunning absence of analysis of black activism and the political thought generated in the context of black struggles for freedom, equality, and justice but also a more general absence of taking race seriously as a historical phenomenon that has profoundly shaped American institutions, politics, and civil society, as well as individual preferences, norms, and ideologies. I will attempt to both substantiate these claims and further develop all three meanings of "in and out of the left" over the next few chapters.

The result of attempting to work out the relationships between blacks and the left is a book unlike any of my other scholarly work, and not just because it is an expansion of a set of lectures as opposed to a manuscript based on a developed research agenda and substantial empirical work. Unlike my past (and future) work, this manuscript is not built upon the empirical analysis of public opinion about race and politics in the United States. Consequently, it does not make use of the extensive statistical analysis that typifies the great majority of my scholarly corpus. Further, this book does not purport to be a taken as either traditional social movement or original historical research (although it mightily and unashamedly relies on the magnificent work of a number of historians). This work is an attempt to systematize reflections on key moments in black political history in order to see what lessons, if any, are relevant for contemporary American politics and democracy.

This book attempts to begin to answer a question that a number of colleagues and friends asked after the publication of my *Black Visions* in 2001. The stylized form of the question was: "Michael, you have analyzed black ideologies and black politics in print, but you have said very little about the status of contemporary black politics and how black politics should be built in the future. How do you think black politics should be built going forward?" Attempting to answer that question has taken more than a decade and three books. In *Not in Our Lifetimes* (2011), I analyzed the weakness of contemporary black politics within a much more complicated political and racial context. In this work I attempt to begin to suggest what is to be done and where we go from here, based on my reflections on the two most significant periods of radical black insurgency of the twentieth century. In the final book, *Reflections on Black Politics in the Early Twenty-First Century* (forthcoming), I discuss how the empirical and theoretical study of black politics in the academy can illuminate pragmatic problems in contemporary American politics and democratic practices. For better or for worse, in that work I return to a more academic mode of analysis.

I hope that this book, however, contributes to the political debate about how to counter the continuing deadly move to the right in this country, and how to accelerate and strengthen the arduous process of rebuilding progressive movements, particularly black movements for justice and equality. We live in dark times—times that have been compared by some to the period of Redemption during the last decades of the nineteenth century when not only were the democratic gains of the nascent labor movement and what Du Bois termed "black Reconstruction" in the South smashed but also an authoritarian regime of state and civil violence was erected throughout the United States (with its roots in the South) to exploit black labor and oppress the entire black population. Jim Crow, or American apartheid, not only oppressed black people throughout the United States but also dealt a crippling blow to the labor movement and other democratic movements fighting for equality and justice. During those dark times, times when the number of lynchings of blacks reached their height and represented a massive violation of human rights within the United States, the foundation was built for later successful radical black movements. In these dark times we need to lay the foundation for a black politics that once again can be a leading edge of the struggle for justice, equality, and democracy.

BLACKS IN AND OUT
OF THE LEFT

Chapter 1

Foundational Myths

Recovering and Reconciling Narratives of Resistance

On August 9, 1931, sixty thousand people, two-thirds of whom were black, marched behind red flags in the streets of Chicago. The march was part of a funeral for three radical black activists who had been shot by the Chicago police a few days earlier. These activists had been involved in the communist-inspired, extremely effective unemployed councils. The economically devastated black neighborhoods on Chicago's Southside proved especially fertile ground for the anti-eviction organizing that was a central component of the radicals' program. Five thousand members of the black community could be mobilized within half an hour to oppose an eviction (Storch 2007). More often than not, evictions were successfully thwarted, with furniture that had been put out on the street by the landlord's minions being returned to the house and utilities turned back on by the mobilized populace. According to Storch's account, parents in danger of being evicted told their children to "run quick and find the reds" (Storch 2007, 113).

For the Communist Party of the United States (CPUSA), Chicago proved to be a rich source of African American members.

Chicago communists also recruited more successfully in the black areas of the city than in other local racial or ethnic communities (Storch 2007). Black membership in the CPUSA's Chicago branch was proportionately larger than in any other chapter—in Chicago the membership was 24 percent black. Perhaps even more surprisingly, in absolute numbers Chicago also had the largest number of black CPUSA members. The more than four hundred black members of the Chicago branch represented nearly six times the membership of the famed Harlem branch (Storch 2007). The large number of black cadres aided the unemployment councils' work—in Chicago the councils had more than a thousand black members.

The successful organizing infuriated Oscar De Priest. De Priest, the first African American elected to Congress during the twentieth century, was a millionaire landlord who was being hurt by the anti-eviction organizing. A member of the Republican Party, De Priest built a career that combined fighting racial discrimination with opposing government aid to the poor. It was in his role as a self-interested exploiter of black renters that he demanded on August 1 that the police stop the anti-eviction organizing. Two days later three organizers were dead. De Priest was typical of a segment of the black middle and upper classes who genuinely acted as strong "race men"—except when their economic interests and those of their patrons were threatened.

Ironically, the leaders of the Communist Party were also disconcerted by the successful organizing of black radicals on the Southside. Chicago's black Communist Party cadres were extremely diverse. Their numbers included doctrinaire Leninists such as the influential Communist leader Harry Haywood, middle-class intellectuals such as the towering literary figure Richard Wright, effective female organizers (whose efforts went largely undocumented by both the CPUSA and scholars), and neighborhood activists. Many black party members across the ideological spectrum were former Garveyites, a status that reinforced the beliefs of white party leaders that the Southside blacks were too independent, too religious, and most of all too nationalist—in short, too embedded in black culture and politics.[1] The dominance of blacks both at the grassroots level and in the leadership of the party and the unemployed councils also concerned the white leadership. Like political organizations of the past and future, both radical and liberal, the Communist Party was worried about being perceived as being "too black." There were also some fairly fundamental differences in perspective between many black organizers and the party's white leadership. Blacks both in and out of the party frequently viewed communism as would the influential Martiniquais poet and activist Aimé Césaire a quarter century later— more concerned about how communism and communists could make conditions better for blacks than about how blacks could aid communism.

The success of communists among blacks during the early 1930s was not confined to just Chicago. The CPUSA led a successful campaign to save the Scottsboro Boys from a legal lynching in Alabama after they had been falsely convicted of raping a pair of white women (who later recanted their testimony and admitted to having had consensual sex with white men). The communist-led international campaign to save the young men gained deep respect and support within black communities across the United States. Nevertheless, over the next few years internal tensions at both the national and local levels led to many purges of blacks on the grounds that they were too interested in black nationalism and the consequent deemphasizing of work among blacks by the Communist Party. These two factors in turn led to the slow withering of support among blacks for the Communist Party over the next three decades, to the extent that when the next mass explosion of black activism occurred the CPUSA would have little visible role to play.

A half century after the police shootings of black radicals in Chicago, four thousand workers led by the Dodge Revolutionary Union Movement (DRUM) shut down Dodge Main on May 2, 1968. This was the first time in fourteen years that the automobile manufacturing plant had been shut down by a strike, either sanctioned or unsanctioned. While some white radicals downplayed the significance of the strike, the *Wall Street Journal* vigorously sounded the alarm. In Detroit, DRUM and its successor organizations were viciously and often violently attacked by a closely coordinated coalition of the police and other state agencies; major employers, particularly the auto industry; and the United Auto Workers (Georgakas and Surkin 1998). Black revolutionaries who managed to both organize black workers and at the same time attract white (and, in Detroit, Arab American) support represented a real and present danger to American capitalism and the hegemony of unions that had reached an often racist accommodation with corporate America.

DRUM and, later, the League of Revolutionary Black Workers, which evolved out of DRUM's work, developed their own unique version of Marxism-Leninism and black nationalism. Like many black radical organizations of that period (most notably its more famous contemporary the Black Panther Party), the league emphasized the need for "organizing alone"—that is, organizing a separate black Marxist organization while fighting for both black liberation and socialist revolution (Georgakas and Surkin 1998, 39). Like many black organizations of the late 1960s and 1970s, the league and DRUM believed that white workers were too reactionary to directly unify with them. What were perceived as entrenched racist attitudes among white workers, combined with the belief that racism among white workers in turn led to more reactionary attitudes toward working-class struggle, convinced black radicals such as the members of DRUM that it was premature to build multiracial organizations.

The league's view on race and organizing did not prevent its cadres from having extremely effective working relations with white workers and activists within the plants as well as more generally in radical coalitions in Detroit. Often league personnel led metropolitan-area-wide multiracial activist coalitions and alliances. League leaders for a brief though important period ran the Wayne State University student newspaper, the *South End,* which had a daily circulation of eighteen thousand. Working with local white radicals, they used the paper to provide a radical viewpoint on a wide range of local, national, and international issues and events. Often most of the paper's daily run would be distributed outside the campus, in Detroit neighborhoods and at various plants. The league also worked in multiclass black united fronts such as the broad coalition opposing police brutality (including police raids on a wide range of black radicals—particularly black nationalists).

Eventually the league would have a significant influence on the national black liberation movement of the 1970s, in at least two different ways. First, organizations that were inspired in part by the example of DRUM and the League of Revolutionary Black Workers formed at universities, auto plants, hospitals, and many other types of workplaces throughout the country—from Palo Alto,

California, to Mahwah, New Jersey. Second, the league expanded its own activities nationwide, and its propaganda apparatus became very sophisticated. The league-produced film *Finally Got the News* was arguably the most influential film produced within the black liberation movement.

The league also led a nationwide campaign demanding reparations for slavery as well as for losses due to the American system of apartheid known as Jim Crow.[2] The league particularly targeted its reparation demands at white religious institutions. Despite extremely hostile attacks from the white media and other institutions, as well as significant internal skepticism within the league itself about the desirability of such a move, the campaign ended up generating at least $200,000.

The league's national work took place within the context of an extremely high level of activity by the black liberation movement well into the 1970s, long after black insurgency had disappeared from the front pages of the nation's newspapers as well as from the minds of most white Americans. The African Liberation Support Committee was the most important organization bringing together wide sectors of the black nationalist and black Marxist wings of the black liberation movement. Not only was it able to mobilize tens of thousands of people (mostly but not exclusively African American) on African Liberation Days during the 1970s, but it also proved to be the most important forum for ideological debate between black nationalists and the growing black socialist movement. This ideological debate would shape not only the black liberation movement during the 1970s but also the nature of the entire New Communist movement within the United States during the same period.

By 1980 black radicalism—both the nationalist and Marxist wings, but particularly the latter—had lost influence, membership, and direction. Black politics would become dominated by black liberals once more, and to an unfortunate degree in the twenty-first century by black liberals who have at least partially embraced neoliberal ideology and agendas. The many reasons for this decline will be discussed in depth in later chapters, but one significant factor was the abandonment of the focus on how black radicalism could help further blacks' quest for justice and liberation, as opposed to how the black movement could be harnessed to build the socialist movement within the United States. As at other times during the twentieth century, this ideological move was accompanied by the twin phenomena of organizations deemphasizing autonomous work in support of black liberation within the United States and the continual purging of black cadres from these organizations due to charges of black nationalism.

These two vignettes of black radical organizing raise three questions that I address in this book. First, what happened to the vibrant black leftist movements that were so influential in African American politics for much of the twentieth century? Second, why is the legacy of these movements relatively unknown among academics and the practitioners of black politics—particularly the younger ones? Third, are there paths for black politics that have been forgotten but which may offer lessons that are applicable today?

A larger question is, why is any of this important? Some say that in 2012 we are living in an age of relative black euphoria. Contrast this with the period from 1993 to 2005, which was one of bitter black disillusionment. As Table 1.1 displays, two-thirds of African Americans in 1993 believed that blacks either would not achieve racial equality in the United States during their lifetime or would never achieve racial equality. This figure steadily rose in

Table 1.1   Black Pessimism on the Likelihood of Achieving Racial Equality

	1993–1994	2000	2003	2004	2005	2008	2009	2010
Unlikely to achieve black racial equality soon	65%	73%	71%	82%	82%	47%	48%	57%

Data compiled from data sets by author. The percentages in the cells represent the combination of those respondents who answered "not in my lifetime" and those who answered that black racial equality would "never" happen in the United States. For more details on the methodology by which this data was produced see Dawson (2011).

the following years, reaching over 80 percent in the aftermath of 2005's Hurricane Katrina. Now, however, the data show that by October 2008 racial optimism had grown dramatically, with more than half of blacks (53 percent) now agreeing that racial equality would be achieved no later than in the near future. This percentage remained high in our 2009 study. By 2010, however, black pessimism once again began to increase. Even so, it was still far below the levels found between 1993 and 2005.

Surely, then, any discussion of the relationship between blacks and the left would be at best a relatively minor historical footnote or perhaps an exercise in nostalgia by aging former activists. After all, goes the argument embraced by conservatives, neoliberals, and many media pundits, the rise in black optimism reflects a changed American reality, one in which there is no longer a need for militant black mobilization because the society is nearly fully open to blacks—at least those who work hard and follow the rules. The election of the first black president is surely all the evidence needed that the days of protest are no longer necessary. Those who do not want to just kick back and enjoy the well-earned rewards of success in a postracial society should focus on helping the less fortunate overcome individual pathologies that lead to some blacks remaining on the bottom; they could also focus on eliminating group pathologies found in certain segments of the black community. Black progress, they argue, will come most rapidly if blacks are directed along the road to entrepreneurship and economic endeavors more generally, and away from the pursuit of political remedies.

Even if for some reason we think the history of black radicalism is important, or we believe that even with the relative optimism of blacks today there remains a strong need for a revitalization of radical versions of black politics, has not David Scott in *Conscripts of Modernity* (2004) given us sufficient reason to be skeptical of a project that attempts to apply lessons from what he calls the "Romantic" period of black politics to the present "tragic" era of black politics? Scott argues that the failures of the postcolonial era (in the United States specifically, the post-civil-rights and post-black-power era) demonstrate that not only were the strategies and tactics associated with the era of worldwide black mobilization fatally flawed at that time and unsuitable for today's conditions, but the aspirations generated during those times are also dangerously inappropriate for the present plight of blacks in the United States and elsewhere. Scott's analysis strongly suggests that there are compelling reasons to believe that the lessons of the past, no matter how accurately identified, would be of little use to black politics today.

Let me suggest several reasons we should pay close attention to this topic. First, there are objective reasons. It is still the case that as of 2010 more than half of African Americans remained racial pessimists, particularly as compared to Americans of other ethnicities. This pessimism has major ramifications for American politics and especially black politics, as it is potentially a source of discontent that can be mobilized into an active opposition (whether nationalist, religious, feminist, progressive, or some combination) to the current political and economic status quo.

My data show that during this period of relative optimism a substantial segment of the black population still believes not only that the promise of the American dream was not meant for them but also that it will not be realized for blacks anytime soon. Therefore it is not surprising that the type of support for social democratic politics that I highlighted in *Black Visions* seems to remain attractive to the residents of at least some black communities (see also Parks and Warren 2009).

Further, blacks have been a population consistently opposed to the war in Iraq.[3] Table 1.2 shows that a solid percentage of African Americans between 2003 and 2005 (the years for which we have data) believed it was proper to protest the war if one disagreed with military intervention, while a substantial majority of white Americans believed it was unpatriotic to protest the war in Iraq. Black opinion has often been far more antiwar than that of other groups (particularly white Americans), as well as far more supportive of (and receptive to) dissenting and radical voices.

More broadly, the combination of intense skepticism about the prospects for racial justice, antiwar sentiment, and an openness to

Table 1.2   Approve Military Action in Iraq?

Approve War?	2003	2004	2005
Blacks	44%	45%	39%
Whites	75%	65%	66%

Data compiled from data sets by author. For more details on the methodology by which this data was produced see Dawson (2011).

social democratic framings of policy issues suggests that there remains a substantial potential for mobilization to progressive causes within most black communities—potentially a richer base for mobilization than can be found in many white communities at this time. Consequently, I argue that from the standpoint of the study of black politics, radical politics, or more generally American politics, the continuing possibilities for black radical mobilization provide rich material for analysis by social scientists interested in radical movements in the United States.

There are also theoretical reasons to pursue this endeavor. For example, there are multiple narratives that seek to explain why the left in the United States collapsed during the 1970s and, more specifically, what role identity politics played in its downfall. It is not a matter of apportioning blame; there is plenty to go around. Rather, if we wish to understand why the progressive social movements of the 1950s, 1960s, and early 1970s gave way to the successful social movements of the right in the 1980s and beyond, we must understand the role of a variety of factors—race and racism, nationalism and separatism, economic disasters in the West, the end of the Vietnam War, misogyny and homophobia, the fragmentation of a universalist left, and the American triumph during the Cold War. It is also about understanding how ideological positions and political practices of the left led, often inadvertently, to the reproduction of structures of racial subordination within the myriad of progressive social movements that came into being during the first three-quarters of the twentieth century. One of the central claims of my work over the years has been that to theoretically understand black politics, or more generally the politics of race, one must understand how the evolving American racial order affects political and social movements, political institutions, worldviews, and preferences. Understanding how the racial order shapes and is shaped by radicalism (as well as other forms of politics) is necessary if we are to untangle theoretical questions about the role race and racial politics played in the rise and fall of radical movements in the twentieth century.

There are normative concerns as well. Certainly, for example, building multiracial political alliances is desirable from the standpoint of the polity. The building of these alliances is not the exclusive province of the left, although blacks have more often been found in left-leaning alliances than in those of the center (and blacks are virtually never a major component of rightist alliances within the United States). It could very well be the case, however, that the lessons on multiracial alliances derived from a study of radical movements may lead to more generally applicable inferences.

Finally, and perhaps most important, is the question of what type of country we want to live in. Is the United States a patriarchal, white-dominated, Christian nation, or is it a liberal, multiracial, religiously tolerant country governed by egalitarian democratic principles? These two concepts of America cannot peacefully coexist.[4] If one wishes for the latter vision, then one needs to agree with Walter Mosley: "The lack of a true understanding of African-American history and its relationship to the rest of the American story keeps the whole nation from a clear understanding and articulation of the present-day political and economic problems that face us all" (Mosley 2000, 13; see also Guinier and Torres 2002). Understanding why African Americans were attracted to leftist, black nationalist, and other radical causes throughout the twentieth century can help us better understand why the political and economic systems and their associated institutions not only were perceived by many blacks to have failed them but in fact did fail them. The failure of American institutions to adequately address African Americans was indicative of their failure to serve large majorities of all Americans. To use Guinier and Torres's (2002) metaphor, when the canary is ill, the miners are in trouble as well.

Let me suggest two lines of argument that combine objective, theoretical, and normative reasons for the study of radical black politics. First, one of the classic questions of American history is why a strong social democratic movement never developed in this country. Relatedly, attention has also been focused on why the United States developed a bifurcated welfare state, in which income-support benefits for the poor are assigned to a different category than the benefits available to all Americans, in contrast to the more unified model found in Western European countries. The role of race in stunting the development of the American welfare state has been profitably examined by several scholars. What I want to argue is that a central but understudied aspect of the story is the inability of the organized American left, particularly its social democratic wing, to successfully incorporate black activists, and more generally its refusal to take on questions of racial justice. This was a critical failure that contributed to the weaknesses of both social democracy and the American welfare state.

Arguably, the Socialist Party was the key organization promoting social democracy during the period in the early twentieth century that was critical in shaping the future development of the left in the United States. The toleration and to some degree promotion of racism within the Socialist Party was critical to the future development of the social democratic left. In its early years the Socialist Party both had a base within white communities and attracted some of the most outstanding members of the pre–World

War I black radical leadership. The party's failure to combat racism within its ranks and more generally within society shaped white and black views about the role of race and racism for decades to come. Not only did this failure lead to long-term weaknesses in American social democracy, it also was one of the factors that encouraged black leftists to turn toward more radical, often Leninist (and much later Maoist) alternatives than otherwise might have been the case.

Black leftists were angered and disgusted by the often outright hostility of the Socialist Party and similar social democratic forces, both toward them personally and toward their focus on fighting against racism and for black liberation (Davies 2008; Haywood 1978; Perry 2009; Solomon 1997). This is another interesting and complementary understanding of the claim that black leftists were driven toward more-radical positions than traditional leftists. As Carole Boyce Davies (2008) so eloquently argues, black communists such as Claudia Jones were to "the left of Karl Marx" because they had to transform traditional male and Eurocentric Marxism, both theoretically and in practice, to eliminate its historical limitations and incorporate patriarchal and racial oppression within its analytical framework. According to multiple generations of black (and other nonwhite) leftist activists, this transformed Marxism was more radical than its original version precisely due to its ability to incorporate a wider array of oppressions that certainly were related to capitalism but could not be fully understood solely within a traditional analysis of capitalism.

Concepts such as "super-exploitation" that flowed from analyses of the oppression of women, colonial subjects, and blacks (leading in turn to concepts such as the triple exploitation of black women, an idea found in Jones's writings from the 1940s) are founded on analyses of separate domains of oppression, such as patriarchy and racial oppression, that intersect with, transform, and are transformed by capitalist oppression. The historical inability of major sectors of the white-dominated left to incorporate these analytical frameworks led to a more radical and often at least partially separate black radicalism. Social democracy in the United States was (and is) doomed to be at best a secondary player in American politics if it cannot incorporate opposition to racial oppression within its theoretical framework or practical program.

Second, from the standpoint of black politics we should remember that the black power movement did not just produce charismatic leaders, radical (and sometimes thuggish) posturing, and violent confrontations with police. Only the civil rights movement transformed more American institutions and led to greater black progress than the black power movement. The civil rights movement mostly successfully took on the extraordinary task of dismantling American apartheid. The black power movement enabled the transformation of public and private American institutions and, in what is perhaps an ironic turn, laid the basis for the modern black middle class's success. It led to the recognition and rooting out of racist practices in both private workplaces and state institutions such as the military. In the wake of that era new institutions would become an enduring part of the American landscape. The black power movement in cities such as Newark, New Jersey; Detroit, Michigan; and Gary, Indiana, contributed to growing black urban electoral strength. The black power era was also a period of political experimentation and innovation. Despite the tragedies and failures of that time, it also fundamentally changed the racial landscape particularly in the political and social sphere. However, the long-term economic results of the black power movement, like those of the civil rights movement, have been disappointing—both movements met with the least success in attempting to improve the economic status of particularly poor African Americans.

Poor African Americans especially still face continued structural disadvantages at the intersections of race and class despite the progress won through the sacrifices of the civil rights and black power movements. In my book *Not in Our Lifetimes* (2011), I document the wide range of substantial racial and socioeconomic disparities still to be found in health care, crime and punishment, and a host of other areas of life. Here I do not intend to go into depth about the circumstances that are the foundation for harsh critiques of the current state of affairs, but it is these conditions that also provide the foundation for the continuing radical edge to black public opinion. There is still a need for a militant wing of black politics to address these disadvantages, as it has become clear over the past three decades that those engaged in "mainstream" politics have proven insufficient to bring about the fundamental change needed to address these problems, and perhaps are uninterested in doing so.

Narratives

In this section I will discuss two somewhat contradictory narratives about U.S. radicalism in the early twentieth century that have shaped the scholarly and political understanding of black politics, its radical wing, and its relationship to the left in the United States. There are three lessons I wish to emphasize from these narratives.

First, the general history of progressive and labor movements, including specifically the history of Marxism in the United States and the history of what is called the New Left, has been until recently whitewashed, and for some scholars this remains the case. This whitewashing not only leads to misapprehension of the nature, scope, and activities of the left in virtually any period of the twentieth century but also makes it extremely difficult to draw scholarly or political lessons from that history. Davies describes this process with respect to major communist leader Claudia Jones:

> How could someone who had lived in the United States from the age of eight, who had been so central to black and communist political organizing throughout the 1930s and 1940s up to the mid-1950s, simply disappear? How could such a popular public figure, an active journalist and public speaker, a close friend of Paul and Eslanda Goode Robeson, a house mate of Lorraine Hansberry, mentored by W. E. B. Du Bois, remain outside of major consideration? (Davies 2007, 1)

Davies's answer is that Jones was "erased" from African American, radical, feminist, and Caribbean histories. As Davies and other black feminist scholars have detailed, this is a phenomenon most acutely observed in relation to black women activists in the United States and elsewhere in the diaspora. It is also a phenomenon observable in relation to many (although not all) black male radicals as well. Harry Haywood and Cyril Briggs are two examples of figures who were important in their time but are now at best footnotes in the historiography of American radicalism; Hubert Harrison is missing entirely from such accounts. The history of the American left is grossly distorted due to this erasure.[5]

Second, not only has the white left historically been complicit in the erasure of black radicals and their contributions from the historical record, but it has also often been openly hostile toward black radicals and their aspirations, ideas, and programs. This was true of both the social democratic left and the Leninist left. The left itself has directly facilitated the distortion of American radical history. Many of the historians who have written about the left have either emerged from or been sympathetic to leftist movements in the United States. Consequently, many but not all have been influenced by the hostility and/or apathy that white-dominated leftist movements have had toward black radicalisms. Indeed, as Davies (2007) documents, Jones's theoretical and programmatic initiatives were met with charges of "reverse chauvinism," particularly from her white female comrades. (Something similar occurred with earlier communists such as Richard Moore.) The later generation of black leftists of the 1960s and 1970s would be called racists by the right and black nationalists by broad segments of the white-dominated left. This hostility has led to an erasure of black radicals and their causes that goes beyond the general censorship and erasure of U.S. left history.

Third, and somewhat separate from the first two points, there was a different path for radical black politics to follow before the massive battles between black leftists, liberals, and nationalists that came to dominate black radical politics from the 1920s through the middle 1960s. In the early twentieth century and from approximately 1966 to 1974, black leftists pursued an organizational strategy that emphasized work among African Americans, as well as working-class struggle, but within all black organizational forms. This path was followed for only a few years in the early 1970s before a return to doctrinaire Marxism—a Marxism less careful about challenging the privileges of white supremacy and patriarchy. It would behoove us to investigate whether the path that, as we shall soon see, was foreclosed in the early twentieth century due to Hubert Harrison's organizational ineffectiveness and misogyny (and the greater skills and charisma of his rivals) offers anything to us today. Given the current state of relations between black movements and progressive movements, as well as the current weakness of black politics itself, is there any value in considering how organizations that are racial in form but radical in content might be effective today, or has the time for their effectiveness passed for good? Let us start this inquiry with a recent version of early twentieth-century American radicalism.

Origins and Roots of the Left

In February 2010, the *New York Times Sunday Book Review* raved about Yale historian Beverly Gage's 2009 book, *The Day Wall Street Exploded: A Story of America in Its First Age of Terror.* The review ends with this quote from Gage's book: "There remains a tendency to think of violence as an anomaly, something outside the American experience, rather than as one of the many ways that Americans have long carried out their political disputes."

I like the book for many of the same reasons that the reviewer cites. Still, I was taken aback by Gage's book for two reasons—reasons that are too typical of much of the scholarship on the American left. First is her (and the reviewer's) comment about how Americans today view political violence as an anomaly. Gage explains, for example, "Nothing in my experience gave me an immediate understanding of why Americans would have been so accustomed to this sort of violence in 1920." She goes on to define *terrorism* as "a form of political violence designed to induce fear and thus destabilize the social order," and she reports that the term is clearly being used in this sense within the American context by "sometime in the first half of the nineteenth century" (Gage 2009, 3–4). What becomes clear, however, is the whiteness of her view not only of political violence in the United States at the end of the nineteenth century and the beginning of the twentieth but also more generally of radical movements of that time.

Gage makes a valid point that Americans at the beginning of the twentieth century would have been well aware of a rising tide of industrial violence in the form of strikes and violent union action, vicious attacks by the state and corporations against miners and other strikers, and violence by anarchists and others on the left. What is stunning is what she misses. Bracketing the 1920 Wall Street bombing was an extraordinary wave of mass violence directed toward blacks between 1919 and 1923—from lynchings to urban riots and outright pogroms. During the Red Summer of 1919 dozens of blacks were killed in Chicago alone, and many times that number in rural Elaine, Arkansas. Entire black neighborhoods were burned to the ground in Longview, Texas; Norfolk, Virginia; and Chicago, Illinois. In Charleston, South Carolina, and Washington, D.C., uniformed white soldiers and/or sailors led the attacks on African Americans.

In 1921 black Tulsa, a community so prosperous by black standards that it was called the "Black Wall Street," was burned down, and at least three hundred blacks were killed when whites attacked. The spark, as was often the case in these affairs, was an alleged assault of a white woman by a black man. The twist was that this time blacks armed and defended themselves, and eventually the National Guard was brought in to disarm them. Two years later a very similar thing happened in Rosewood, Florida.

These atrocities were embedded in a larger wave of violence that originated in the South as an attempt to keep blacks from exercising their political rights immediately after the Civil War (the Ku Klux Klan was launched in 1866). More than two thousand blacks would be lynched between 1882 and 1905, with the greatest numbers coming after 1892, and lynching would continue well into the 1940s. The period with the greatest number of lynchings coincided with black disenfranchisement in the South starting in Mississippi in 1891 and ending in Georgia in 1906. Although, as noted earlier, allegations of rape by black males were usually cited as the reason for any given lynching, lynchings were a weapon of terror aimed at suppressing black political power and, as the great antilynching champion Ida B. Wells observed, at dispossessing successful blacks of their property. Indeed, the initial wave of violence against blacks during the Reconstruction fits Gage's definition of terrorism, as lynching was used first to undermine and then to destroy the democratic southern governments that were established after the Confederate defeat and often featured heavy black participation. The wave of violence against blacks that occurred during the period Gage wrote about was aimed not at destabilizing a political order but at reinforcing one—the racial order known as Jim Crow. The perpetrators of the violence aimed to solidify the political, social, and economic subjugation of blacks not only in the South but throughout the rest of the United States. This political violence was terrorism—albeit state-sanctioned, and sometimes even state-sponsored.

Of course the Haymarket riot preceded the Wall Street bombing by a generation, but white supremacist terror directed against Southern blacks preceded even Haymarket.[6] Many of us think of the term *race riot* as being associated with the urban disturbances of the 1960s and afterward. The race riots of the first half of the twentieth century, however, in places such as Tulsa, Chicago, Rosewood, Springfield, Illinois and many other localities were much more violent. Yet historical narratives of terrorism in the United States, including Gage's, are silent on the question of terrorism directed at blacks and other subordinated communities of color even when the level of violence is equivalent to that of European pogroms and had clear political motivations and results.

The objection to this critique could be that Gage's book is not about racial violence but about political violence and general radical politics in the United States in the first few decades of the twentieth century. However, Gage's racial blindness goes deeper than selection of material. She mentions the Ku Klux Klan once, but not in relation to terror directed at African Americans; rather, she discusses it in regard to the lynching of a Jewish factory manager, Leo Frank, in New Orleans in 1915. The Frank lynching was a horrendous miscarriage of justice, but it is bizarre that the only mention of the Klan's terrorism in the South references the lynching of a white American. She mentions lynching approximately five times in the book: once with regard to Frank, twice referring to western miners, and a couple of times metaphorically in reference to the state repression that descended on radicals of all stripes during and after World War I—but never in reference to African Americans, who were overwhelmingly its victims.

More generally, blacks are not a part of her story of the left in New York and America. The one time blacks are mentioned it is in passing, where Gage suggests that the Great Migration was misnamed, as "it was just one migration among many" that brought a population influx to New York City (p. 21). But this massive migration of blacks from the South to northern cities including New York reshaped the social, economic, and political fabric of those cities such as New York, including their radical political landscape.

The absence of African Americans is problematic for Gage's narrative in several ways. First, political violence at the turn of the century has to be put in the context of the endemic racial violence of the time. One reason Americans of that period may have been relatively acclimated to political violence was the high and continuing levels of racial violence that occurred in all areas of the country. And racial violence is not just a matter for American social history; the violence was *political,* aimed at maintaining a severely oppressive racial order that itself had political as well as economic and social elements. The extremely violent 1906 Atlanta riot not only was instigated by local papers that were trying to get their candidates elected governor but also was directly tied to the campaign to disenfranchise black Georgia citizens—the last Deep South black citizens to be disenfranchised. The urban pogroms were not only about competition for jobs and housing—political enough in their own right—but also about what the late political theorist Judith Shklar called "standing." White Americans at the time objected to black economic, social, and political enfranchisement because they argued explicitly that it undermined *their* standing as citizens (Dawson 2001; Arnesen 1994). Thus, uniformed black veterans of World War I were particularly targeted for violence—sometimes being pulled off trains by white mobs, including mobs of uniformed white veterans, and killed. More generally, African Americans who stood up for their citizenship rights were a target for white terrorists.

Second, while Gage's book discusses the growth and repression of leftist movements in the United States, it overlooks how antiblack racial violence acted as fuel for black political activists and led to an increase in membership for the National Association for the Advancement of Colored People (NAACP), the African Blood Brotherhood (ABB), the Communist Party of the United States, the Socialist Party (SP), and of course the Garvey movement, which was the largest black urban political movement in U.S. history. It also helped to fuel a black cultural revolution that would include the Harlem Renaissance. Not only did the racial violence aimed at blacks lead blacks to form their own radical organizations, but it also influenced blacks such as Du Bois, Chandler Owen, and A. Philip Randolph to affiliate with the Socialist Party and some such as Briggs and Haywood to eventually join the Communist Party.

I focus on Gage's book because it is a very recent and well-regarded work, published by an academic press, that continues to promote a racially narrow view of American radicalism. Even works such as *Marxism in the United States* (Buhle 1991) that consciously attempt to integrate some of this history into a more overarching and inclusive narrative of American radicalism treat black radicalism as a sideshow.[7] While some might say this choice is at least debatable when it comes to the history of the early decades of the twentieth century, I argue that leaving out these events results in an important gap for any work attempting to explain the use of political violence in any era of American history, and it is definitely not a viable approach for explaining American radicalism in the era of the civil rights and black power movements.

Part of the problem with narratives that leave out black radicalism often involves the definition of radicalism they adopt. Implicitly they assume that radical movements are predominantly white, because the black population was considered to be inherently backward and a drag on the working-class. This viewpoint can be found repeatedly within the New Left. Second, they place the engine for radical change within the white male proletariat, making labor conflict the focus of much of the historiography. Anti-lynching struggles led by individuals such as Ida B. Wells, the political activity of the woman suffrage movements, and the massive struggles against racial violence are all relegated to at best a secondary role even though historians such as Geoff Eley have shown that the role of the traditional Euro-American proletariat was not as central to either the growth of capitalism or the resistance to capitalism and imperialism as has been traditionally portrayed in histories of the left. One cannot study leftist movements in the United States without examining how the racial and capitalist orders are mutually constitutive and without understanding how, for example, the racial reign of terror reinforced and facilitated the reign of terror directed against worker movements (including those of predominantly white workers).

Before I move to a narrative on early black radicalism, I want to discuss a set of related concerns that bridge black and white narratives. Overt racism within the early twentieth-century American left had a profound effect on the racial makeup of the American left, but it is not often analyzed in mainstream discussions of American radicalism. When it *is* addressed by scholars or activists, frequently they claim that "that was then, this is now," and that racism within the left no longer need be a central concern. However, racism within organizations such as the Socialist Party and later the CPUSA shaped not only blacks' views of the left (as did the much better documented, often intense, and sometimes official racism found within the unionized labor movement) but also how white radicals viewed the radical potential of blacks and other groups of color.

Another continuity I want to highlight here involves the downplaying of race as a shaping force of American life, whether politically, socially, or economically. Consequently, within the predominantly white sector of the left, the concerns of blacks and other people of color about racial justice were often either viewed as a distraction, a minor issue to be settled after socialist victory, or with outright hostility. One result was an extraordinarily blind and crude view of black nationalism. For example, as late as the 1970s, *after* efforts of black nationalists such as Malcolm X and black nationalist organizations had contributed to bringing radical change to the United States, a leader of the CPUSA was still declaring that all forms of nationalism were reactionary and designed to divide the working class. White leftists' hostile attitudes toward black nationalism in the last third of the century were virtually identical to such attitudes in the first third, and they are often present today in what passes for a progressive movement.

Outright racism was particularly prevalent in the Socialist Party, which was one of the two key early left formations in the country. Philip Foner described the range of racial views within the Socialist Party as very broad. They "ran the gamut from 'outright racist advocacy of white supremacy' . . . to the position that 'the Socialist party should conduct a consistent and persistent struggle against racism'" (Perry 2009, 142). The first view, advocating white supremacy, was all too prevalent within the SP. In 1902 Victor Berger, who eight years later would be the first Socialist Party member elected to Congress, said, "Negroes and mulattoes constitute a lower race." Socialist theoretician Ernest Untermann stated, "I am determined that my race shall be supreme in this country and the world" (Perry 2009, 142–143). Berger in 1908 declared the United States was a "white man's country" and that it would be socialism's job to ensure that it remained so, for if not, it would become "a black and yellow country in a few generations." Even presidential candidate Eugene Debs, a racial liberal by Socialist Party standards, stated there was "no negro problem apart from the general labor problem," and he believed that even to bring up the question of black equality would divide the working class.

In truth, the working class was already divided. It was divided by the frequent lynching of African Americans and the refusal of the white-dominated left to take up the struggle against lynching. It was divided by racially segregated communities—communities whose racial boundaries were violently policed by white working-class thugs. It was divided by lily-white unions that relentlessly attempted to purge craft and other trades of black workers. Yet the refrain that speaking about or organizing around racial justice would divide the working class would be heard time and time again. It was not just the early socialists who championed this view. It was heard within the CPUSA during most of its long history (the 1930s were a partial exception). In a much later era, so-called Marxists affiliated with the new communist movement of the 1970s marched with the Klan against busing in Boston in the name of working-class unity. And today there is a long list of race-related issues that cannot be discussed, the claim goes, because they too will divide the progressive movement—this was often the case with the horrific events surrounding Hurricane Katrina (Dawson 2011). Public opinion data also demonstrate the continued deep racial cleavage (Dawson 2011). The question is how to overcome the racial chasms that are still a central factor in American political life.

Debs would go on to say in 1904 that the Socialist Party had "nothing special to offer the negro" (Perry 2009, 144). He was right. Banning Socialist Party organizing around the interests of particular groups was not a uniform policy, however. There were special programs and sections for the organizing of both immigrants and women. One key reason, according to Perry, that there was robust organizing around women's issues within the Socialist Party was that at the dawn of the century there was a strong, organized, and militant women's movement that was able to directly and indirectly influence groups such as the Socialist Party to step up their own efforts. There was no consistently strong, autonomous black radical movement that could force the Socialist Party to recognize the necessity of supporting black cadres' attempts to organize in support of black liberation. It is also the case that whether we are talking about pressuring the state or the organizations of the left, black progress has been greatest when there was an organized, independent black political movement. The SP made sporadic and inconsistent efforts to organize blacks, but support was often discriminatory and weakly resourced, and the activists who engaged in such work were commonly viewed with suspicion. And from the 1910s well into the 1980s, blacks would be purged from putatively leftist organizations for being nationalists.

This experience with white-dominated organizations is one of the reasons Hubert Harrison emphasized independent black radical organizing. Uniting workers (or, more generally today, progressives) could not occur without confronting the ills of the racial order (Perry 2009, 162). The debate that raged among black Socialist Party members such as Du Bois and Harrison would be replicated fifteen years later in the CPUSA and in the 1960s and 1970s within black, Asian American, and Latino radical organizations. The debate was centered on how multiracial organizations should organize their work among blacks. Du Bois took the position that leftist organizations should not be internally segregated, with separate committees for blacks. Harrison and many others who came after him made the counterargument that having black subgroups within the Socialist Party would help overcome the black community's suspicion of white organizations and was a perfectly reasonable organizational strategy (Perry 2009, 169–172).

A similar debate was being vigorously waged within the international socialist movement at the time. The Jewish Bund, formed in czarist Russia in 1897, was one of the founding groups of the Russian Social Democratic Labor Party (the precursor to the Communist Party of the Soviet Union) in 1898. For a period the Bund was considered the sole representative of Jewish members of the party, but by 1903 the party decided to ban all such formations, leading to the withdrawal of the Bund (which would rejoin the Russian party in 1906). The debate over Bundism would become an integral part of Marxist debates over the next several decades, and blacks, Latinos, and Asian Americans would often be called Bundists in the 1960s and 1970s for advocating the organization of racially or ethnically based units within socialist organizations to conduct specific work within a given racial or ethnic group. The Bund was not an unreasonable analogy (although many of the people who were called Bundists had to look up the reference, which was relatively obscure). Like the Bund, black organizations such as Students Organized for Black Unity (SOBU), the Black Workers Congress, and the Congress of African People; Latino organizations such as the East Coast–based Young Lords Party and the Southwest- and California-based August 29th Movement;

and Asian American organizations such as the Red Guards, I Wor Kuen, and the East Wind and Japan Town Collectives not only were formed prior to the most of the Marxist organizations that they later were folded into but also often would form the backbone of both the membership and leadership of the later organizations. Most white activists of this period were unaware of the depth and influence that these racially and ethnically based organizations had within their respective communities, but the results of their organizing were highly visible and effective. Even within these organizations, however, the question of how to organize work among nonwhite communities was a source of intense strife. As noted, eventually most of these organizations either merged into multiracial communist organizations (which over time became increasingly resistant to either internal or external radical formations organized along racial lines) or dissolved.

Harrison's point was not to promote segregation within organizations such as the Socialist Party but to preserve black autonomy within these organizations, particularly when it came to formulating strategies and goals for work among blacks. By the 1930s, of course, Du Bois had come to a similar position, but Harrison was one of the first of what would become hundreds of black leftists who would fight this battle in multiracial organizations for the remainder of the century. By 1912 Harrison had lost this battle within the SP; there would be a temporary revival of work aimed at blacks years later under the prodding of Randolph and Owen, but by the mid-1920s they had distanced themselves from the party, and this line of work would never be active again. This pattern repeated itself on a more protracted scale within the CPUSA between the 1920s and 1930s.

Harrison argued that supporting African Americans was "the crucial test of Socialism's sincerity" (Perry 2009, 180), and by

1913 Du Bois publicly agreed (Perry 2009, 214). But socialism at the beginning of the last century failed the test.

Origins and Roots of Black Radicalism

During the period that Gage discusses, black radicalism was growing throughout the United States, especially in New York City. Throughout the twentieth century black radicals shared many of the same beliefs and practices that distinguished them from more liberal and social democratic left formations, black or otherwise. They tended to identify with the more militant versions of Marxism and with revolutionary thinking more generally. Black radicals insisted on the centrality and revolutionary potential of African American demands and movements and often embraced the right to self-determination for blacks within the United States.[8] They embraced the right to armed self-defense and did not rule out the use of revolutionary violence, as both the Socialist Party did in the early part of the century and the CPUSA did in the civil rights and black power era. The main narrative of black radicalism (much of which I still believe to be accurate) holds that the great A. Philip Randolph and his colleague Chandler Owen's brief and ultimately ineffective sojourn in the Socialist Party represents the tragic failure of the organized social democratic wing of the left to recruit and retain African Americans. Consequently, the black left would never be deeply engaged with the more moderate wings of the white left.

The result, or so the narrative goes, was that by the early 1920s we see dynamics within black movements that would persist in one form or another through the first three-quarters of the century. The battles between the black nationalist Marcus Garvey, the socialist Randolph, and the liberal (at the time) Du Bois set the stage for the century-long conflict between black nationalists, black liberals, and blacks in multiracial leftist organizations that was to dominate black radical movements for much of the century, except for brief periods in which one faction dominated, as the liberals did during the civil rights movement.

The history is of course more complicated and in some ways more tragic than this synopsis suggests, with some missing elements as well as some that changed over the course of the century. For example, after the early 1920s the black socialists faded from sight, to be replaced by the black communists of the 1930s and by a variety of types of black leftists and radical nationalists in the late 1960s and most of the 1970s. And this narrative does not incorporate either the organizing black women were doing in black communities via radical organizations such as the Liberty League and the Universal Negro Improvement Association (UNIA) or the battles these women were having with racism within the predominantly white women's movement and with sexism within the black movement. An emblematic figure is Ida B. Wells. As noted, Wells was the most effective antilynching organizer in the country during the early years of the twentieth century, she was well respected within the black movement, and she was a member of the Niagara movement, the precursor to the NAACP. Yet she and Monroe Trotter were the only leading members of the Liberty League who were not invited to participate in the founding of the NAACP. While Trotter and the founders both agreed that he was too nationalistic for the new multiracial organization, Wells was a different matter. One key white founding member of the NAACP, Mary White Ovington, had very little use for Wells and was dismissive of black women in general. She said that black women were "ambitious for power, often jealous, very sensitive, [but] they get things done." These racist attitudes were matched by Du Bois's sexist statement that "nothing more than membership was expected of her in the NAACP" (Dawson 2001, 137). Thus at the beginning of modern black radicalism we see black women who were doing critical work in a variety of political and civic arenas but had to fight for recognition and leadership from both black men and white women. Furthermore, this battle has been significantly "erased," to use Carole Boyce Davies's phrase, from the history of black radicalism and thus from the history of American radicalism. Not only has this erasure led to a crippling of our understanding of black radicalism's history and hampered our ability to build black radical movements, but it has also facilitated the reproduction of oppressive systems of patriarchy and homophobia within black movements other than those led by black feminists.

Another missing element (albeit one that the work of Davies, Winston James, Kelley, Perry, and others has brought more to the fore over the past several years) has been the contributions of West Indian activists to black leftism from the early years through the middle part of the twentieth century. The erasure of figures such as communist leader Claudia Jones, who worked against the intersection of racism and sexism within the CPUSA, leads to an inadequate placement of U.S. black radical movements in the context of U.S. imperialism. It often leads to a type of American exceptionalism that privileges the experiences of and lessons from U.S.-based movements and assumes that those movements should and do provide the template for black movements internationally—at least those located outside the African continent. It sometimes also leads to black radicals being insufficiently cognizant of their responsibilities to movements generated by those who are oppressed by various aspects of U.S. foreign policy and capitalism.

There was, in fact, a twentieth-century black radical organization that emphasized black self-reliance, took an anti-imperialist stance toward the Western powers, called for armed self-defense, emphasized the need to be independent of both major political parties, promoted third world solidarity and placed the struggle of blacks within the United States within the context of the worldwide struggle against Western imperialism, and discussed the choice between the ballot and the bullet. For some readers such a political platform may evoke memories of the Nation of Islam (NOI) circa 1960, or perhaps Malcolm X's Organization of Afro-American Unity in the year before his death (1964); the African Blood Brotherhood of the early twentieth century would also be a reasonable guess. There are parallels to the Black Panther Party of 1967 and the African Liberation Support Committee of the mid- to late 1970s as well. Actually, however, it was the platform of the Liberty League in 1917, the organization founded by St. Croix immigrant and Harlem black radical leader Hubert Harrison.

Harrison saw the question of racial oppression as central to both American democracy and the successful growth of an American left movement. He argued, "Politically, the Negro is the touchstone of the modern democratic idea. . . . [A]s long as the Color Line exists, all the perfumed protestations of Democracy on the part of the white race . . . [are] down right lying (Perry 2009, 5). Harrison, who was forced out of the Socialist Party for being too concerned about work with blacks, came to the conclusion that many other black radicals would come to over the next fifty years: that American socialists were essentially white nationalists, "race first and class after" (Perry 2009, 7). Thus he argued that blacks needed to organize independently until white nationalism no longer dominated American socialism.

Harrison also was critical of the black middle class and anticipated both Marxists and Malcolm X in his class analysis of "house
Negroes" versus "field Negroes," using those terms as Malcolm X
would half a century later. Even though Harrison had split from
the socialists and argued for black organizational autonomy, he still
saw the racialized economy as a central feature of black oppression.
He argued that black oppression was situated in four main categories of human relationships—economic, social, political, and civic.
He argued that economic relationships were most important for
understanding black oppression, because "as long as white men
can be taught to believe that the presence of black men threatens
their means of existence, so long will their general attitude be
one of enmity. So long as the fallacy of economic fear survives, so
long will economic competition create race prejudice" (Perry
2009, 158). He argued that at least as long as the perception persisted among white workers that white supremacy was in their
economic interest, independent black organizing was necessary.

A key critique that Harrison had of leaders such as Du Bois and
Randolph is one that has repeatedly been made in every decade
within not only black radical movements but radical politics more
generally. Harrison argued that Randolph and Du Bois erred by
having "generally gone at the problem from the wrong end . . .
they have begun at the top when they should have begun at the
bottom" (Perry 2009, 271). For Harrison, the only sure way to
build a movement was from the bottom up—black people needed
unity of purpose. In later radical parlance and practice, what Harrison was describing was a black united front—a multiclass formation of African Americans working together toward common
ends. To establish such a front, what would be needed, and what
he saw developing in Harlem, to use his own words, was "race

consciousness" (Perry 2009, 278). Anticipating the argument of the Black Panther Party, which declared that it was "national in form, socialist in content," Harrison argued that it would be through organizing around race that blacks would be fully brought into the working-class movement.

Harrison, Wells, Garvey, the black communists, socialists such as Randolph, and Du Bois as well as Trotter were all products of what was by the early twentieth century a fully developed civil society and black public sphere with leftist, feminist, nationalist, and liberal elements. It included men and women, and black immigrants such as West Indians. They tried to influence white publics (Wells, Du Bois, and Harrison, for example, all saw that as part of their task). This early, lively counterpublic was established institutionally not only in churches, lyceums (the word Harlemites used at the time for debate clubs and similar public forums), block clubs, and literary clubs, all of which would become traditional and foundational components of the black public sphere and civil society, but also in pamphlets, newspapers, public lectures (which could draw several hundred), and oratory on street corners—the last of these being an art that Harrison pioneered. Many of the key leaders of this period such as Garvey and Randolph, following Harrison's example, used street corner oratory as a critical means for building their reputations. By 1917 there was a flourishing of radical black newspapers. Harrison's *Voice* was first, quickly followed by Owen and Randolph's *Messenger,* Briggs's *Crusader,* and Garvey's *Negro World.* The women and men who built these institutions and black civil society more generally had both amazing gifts and all-too-human weaknesses. These weaknesses, as well as their strengths, would contribute to how the black radical movement was shaped over the next several decades. Black radicalism was highly developed within the context of an even more developed black civil society at the same time that American radicalism was attempting to establish itself within twentieth-century America. Most of these activists would either continue to follow the path of black nationalism or take a path that pursued black liberal and/or radical politics within multiracial organizations.

Why did what I call the "third path"—the path that sought to fight for human emancipation from within black radical organizations deeply embedded within black communities and movements—largely disappear for forty years, with the brief exception of the African Blood Brotherhood? This is a question I address over the next two chapters, but some preliminary thoughts are in order. The demise of the Garvey movement as a mass force within black politics seriously crippled black nationalism as a force within black radical politics. Black nationalism did not provide an organizational path to autonomous black radicalism at this time, as it would do in the second period of black insurgency several decades later. In addition, no third-path organization, including the Liberty League and the ABB, really established itself as a national force in black politics. The result was that by the time of Garvey's imprisonment in 1923, there was no longer a third path. The two available paths were that of nationalist organizations such as Garvey's UNIA (and later the Nation of Islam) or that of the white-dominated multiracial socialist organizations. The civil rights movement would provide the first organizational basis for such a third path, albeit largely led by radical black liberals. Emerging from the civil rights movement were the organizations of the black power era, some of which for the first time in decades fully captured the politics and organizational forms pioneered by Harrison and his followers.

Why did Garvey succeed when Harrison did not? There were reasons related to Harrison's character and lack of political sophistication. His misogyny was a factor as well. As in most black organizations, black women played critical roles in maintaining and building the Liberty League, and Harrison lost several women to Garvey's UNIA, including those who were more socialist in orientation than nationalist. Garvey was able to attract a number of women who had worked with the Liberty League and its paper, the *Voice,* due in no small part to the UNIA's focus on organizing around black women's issues. Harrison was also organizationally and financially inept, which is disastrous for organization building. He had a similar lack of the skills needed to promote his organization. Further, Garvey was also much better at incorporating various aspects of black culture as well as recruiting black religious leaders—neither of which seemed to much concern Harrison. Thus, the far more organizationally sophisticated Garvey, Randolph, and others were able to build on Harrison's success and divide the institutional space that Harrison once occupied.

While Harrison's shortcomings and the strengths of his rivals contributed to the disappearance of the third path, there were broader reasons as well. Many black nationalists and socialists were attracted to the potential for allies and the multiple resources provided by white socialist organizations. For another, Garvey knew how to use ritual to generate deep black pride and support. The marches, uniforms, and other activities generated a sense of black and organizational solidarity. Thus Garvey was able to attract both wide and deep activist support *and* mass support.

Cyril Briggs and his organization, the African Blood Brotherhood, along with its paper, the *Messenger,* carried the torch of the third wave for a few years, until the group was fully swallowed by the CPUSA; by the early 1920s it had ceased all independent organizing among blacks. The disappearance of the ABB signaled the absence of an independent, organized black leftist presence within black politics and American radicalism. White-dominated organizations would be the main vehicle for promoting leftist ideas and programs within black communities. Many black cadres of these organizations would prove more than equal to the task of fighting for black liberation in multiracial leftist organizations, but quite a few walked away frustrated with what they believed to be organizational constraints preventing them from pursuing the best strategies and tactics in support of black liberation.

The example of Hubert Harrison reminds us that much remains to be uncovered if we are to understand twentieth-century black politics. Which paths were open at which times? What lessons, if any, can be learned from paths not taken? How would black politics during the 1940s and 1950s have been different if there had been an organized, independent black radical presence?

Conclusion: Reconstructions

Harrison, Randolph, Owen, Haywood, Briggs, and Wright, as well as George Padmore and Harold Cruse—the list goes on—all ended up eventually either walking away from white-led leftist organizations or being purged from them. In many cases it was a "You're fired!" "No, I quit!" situation. In the early and middle parts of the twentieth century, black radicals tried to work with white radicals within the latter group's organizations. But after blacks in both the Socialist and Communist Parties were called "niggers" by their comrades and black women domestic workers were told by their white women employers that they were too "backward" to join the radical movement, most ended up leaving, bitterly renouncing not so much socialism as the white socialists and their organizations. Why? Because they all came to the conclusion, even Du Bois in his own tardy way, that mainstream socialists were first and foremost white nationalists. If black radicals were to preserve any dignity and usefully defend and fight for their communities, they would have to act as at least quasi black nationalists themselves. Black organizational autonomy was required to fight white supremacy within American radicalism.

Because of this history, most of the major white radical organizations would end up on the sidelines when militant liberal mass movements emerged out of the fields, cities, and campuses of the South, to be swiftly followed by a radical fury emerging from the ghettos, barrios, and Chinatowns of the urban North and West. While those later movements are relatively well known and somewhat present in the accounts of 1960s and 1970s American radicalism, unlike the earlier history, even these later movements are the subject of contentious debate, particularly with regard to the question of what role black and other nontraditional working-class movements had in leading to the collapse of American radicalism.

Chapter 2

Power to the People?

Immediately after Martin Luther King Jr.'s assassination, Chicago mayor Richard J. Daley claimed King had been a communist.[1] How could any elected official, especially the mayor of a city with a very large black population, make such a claim during an extraordinary dangerous time? One hundred American cities were burning as a result of the mass black uprisings that occurred after the assassination. But Daley could make such an inflammatory statement because from 1920 to 1970 millions of white Americans found it easy to believe that only a communist would advocate for black equality.

To many, this charge was especially believable if, unlike King, the one advocating for black equality was white. Early in the century blacks began paying attention to charges of the alleged linkage between communism and advocacy on behalf of justice for blacks. This attention led not only to many alliances with leftist forces but also to many black activists adopting various forms of leftist radicalism. These activists viewed black radicalism as a tool to be used in the service of black liberation. The simple truth was that, particularly during the first half of the twentieth century, a substantial proportion of whites openly advocating for black equality *were* communists and their allies. And many communists, both black and white, were heroes who suffered greatly for their deep commitment to racial equality.

The main force winning substantial if incomplete equality for blacks in America, however, was the black mass struggle for freedom. The black freedom struggle faced horrific levels of violence from the state and white civil society, both in the South and in the North, in what can only be called a century-long war to maintain the racial order and white supremacy. In this war, white allies were sorely lacking. The white working class all too often chose its racial interests over its class interests. Even working white women often chose race over class or gender (Biondi 2003; Gilmore 2008; Solomon 1997). More precisely, disadvantaged whites, men and women, saw their class, racial, and gender interests as being identical for all practical purposes, given their submersion in an ideology of white supremacy that portrayed disadvantaged blacks as the worst threat to both their status privilege and their material interests. Worse, those struggling for racial justice in both the South and the North had to fight an unholy alliance of corporate America, white civil society, and the state.[2] Even in the face of this concerted opposition, black radical activism grew in black communities during two distinct eras in the twentieth century. In both eras black radicals challenged white supremacy and searched for allies in the quest for black liberation. This chapter asks what lessons can be learned from analyzing these two peaks of black radical organizing.

In Chapter 1, I argued that the study of black radicalism was important from both scholarly and normative perspectives. I also argued that the general history of progressive and labor movements, and in particular the history of Marxism in the United States and the history of what is called the New Left, has been whitewashed. This whitewashing, in which the white left was complicit, not only has led to misapprehension of the nature, scope, and activities of the left in the twentieth century but also makes it extremely difficult to draw scholarly or political lessons from that history. Finally, I argued that a third path for radical black politics to follow developed before the massive battles between black leftists, black liberals, black nationalists, and (later in the century) black feminists came to dominate black radical politics. This third path, which later would become a significant feature of the black power era's black radical organizing, was marked by the formation of black organizations that claimed to fuse work for black liberation with what they saw as some form of socialist organizing. This stood in contrast to the dominant organizational form of the period 1920–1955, when black leftists were mostly found within multiracial left organizations, primarily the Communist Party of the United States of America.

In this chapter I begin providing evidence in support of these claims, and I ask what can be learned from studying the differences and similarities between the two most intense periods of twentieth-century black radicalism. One central difference between the two periods is that in the first, the one during which the CPUSA dominated black leftist organizing, black radicals were concentrated in a single multiracial, doctrinaire communist organization. In contrast, during the black power era black radicals experimented with a number of different organizational and ideological mixes, including what I labeled in the first chapter "third path" organizations and ideologies. Does this difference, as well as other differences between the two periods, offer any lessons for contemporary black and radical politics?

In this chapter I examine the centrality of race in the left's development. I also demonstrate how the left's consistent mistakes on race directly led to failures in grassroots organizing and in building leftist organizations. The racism of the Socialist Party, highlighted in the last chapter, led to the social democratic vacuum within black radicalism and provided opportunities for Leninist and nationalist alternatives. I will also show how the vital and relatively new understanding of the black freedom struggle characterized by Jacquelyn Dowd Hall as the "long civil rights movement" was mirrored historically by, and intertwined with, an equally long and vibrant process of black radicalism—an element that until very recently has been absent from histories of both the civil rights era and the black power movement (Hall 2005). The modern civil rights and black power movements were directly shaped by events that occurred between the founding of the modern U.S. left in the 1920s and the advent of the Cold War and the anti-Red terror.

First, however, let me say a few words about this chapter's title. One key difference between the two periods is how black radicals conceptualized "the people," "power," and "power to the people." Who are "the people"? This was not an abstract issue for those who debated this question. It profoundly affected, for example, organizational and alliance strategy. During the two eras being examined, "the people" were defined differently by various movements and tendencies within these movements. For example, one black nationalist scholar told me at the time of the Million Man March in 1995 that he believed that some black people, because of their politics, did not belong in the black nation—echoing a common view that he like many other nationalist veterans from the second era continued to hold. Second, particularly during the black power era, what was meant by "power to the people" was hotly contested. Not only was the concept of "the people" at issue, but so was the concept of "power." Did "power" mean the type of power generated through the electoral control of one's community, the economic power generated by the same community, or the type of power gained through working-class revolution? This debate would continue until the decline of radical black politics and the emergence of neoliberal hegemony seemed to foreclose all but the most narrow and apolitical conceptions of "power."

During the first period of black radicalism, after the downfall of the Garvey movement, the CPUSA had hegemonic influence as a radical presence in many black communities. Most black radicals defined "the people" as blacks in the United States, blacks elsewhere, the other "darker races" (to use the terminology of the times), and "class-conscious" white workers. In practice, black Marxists (with a few notable exceptions) focused on black liberation and had as many, if not more, doubts about white workers as they had about the black middle class, which at the time was misnamed the "black bourgeoisie."

During the black power era, very approximately 1965–1975, "the people" were defined much less consistently among black radicals. No single ideology dominated. Not only were there differences between, for example, black leftists, black nationalists, and black feminists about who constituted the people, but within each tendency there were nontrivial differences. For nationalists, did other people of color constitute part of the people? The answer within many of the politically oriented nationalist organizations was yes, but not among cultural nationalists. Among black Marxists the status of both white workers and the black middle class was hotly debated. Debates among black feminists also occurred and sometimes manifested over concerns about how much time should be spent on reaching out to white women. The experience with the Communist and Socialist Parties in the earlier period of black radicalism did much to fuel the debates about how to define who constituted the people in the black power era and later.

As for "power to the people," leftist movements in the United States have been about the acquisition of political power, whether that is explicitly acknowledged or not. But the demand for power, whether electoral, economic, or other, has repeatedly been made on behalf of a wide variety of groups far beyond the various configurations of the classic proletariat promoted by the traditional left. Activists from the LGBT, black, women's, Native American, Chicano, Puerto Rican, and Hawaiian communities, along with many others, have all demanded political power.[3] The form of political power being sought has varied as well. The modern Native American demand was for sovereignty—a type of political power closest to the goals of traditional national movements. Some black nationalists also demanded separate statehood through the political establishment of a black state. Many radicals of color, both nationalists and leftists, called for community control over the political structure and economy of their own communities— a very different concept.

There has also often been significant tension within the black movement over the means through which political power could be achieved, a tension caught most notably in the title of Malcolm X's speech "The Ballot or the Bullet." There has been relatively little disagreement about the need for black power. Liberals such as King, classic black nationalists such as Garvey, and black Marxists such as the leaders of DRUM all advocated for black power even if some, such as King, believed that the use of the term *black power* was counterproductive.[4] Still, there has always been significant disagreement about what means would be used to achieve power.[5] Especially salient were the debates over whether to rely on the electoral system and what, if any, moral or practical use there was for political violence as a means for gaining black liberation. Further, during many periods, including slavery and the black power era, there have also been debates among those advocating violence about what form of violence best served the needs of black liberation (Dawson 2001). During the run-up to the Civil War, for instance, a substantial segment of black activists supported the use of violence to achieve political ends, but by no means all did. It should be noted that these debates were salient not just for black radical movements but more generally for both black politics and progressive movements within the United States.

We must remember that there were some common threads between the two key periods of black radical insurgency. Black activists were insistent on what Karen Ferguson called an "alternative vision of liberty"—one of the black visions I have discussed elsewhere at length. They were just as insistent in their support for the principle of self-determination, the cornerstone of black political thought throughout much of the nineteenth and twentieth centuries (Ferguson 2007; Dawson 2001).

However, apart from these similarities, there was less continuity between these two periods of black radicalism than one might expect, largely due to what I call "the sundering"—the decade between 1945 and 1955, in which black racial activists became isolated from other activists in a variety of domestic and international domains. Delineating the similarities and differences in black radicalism during the two periods of radical upsurge offers some lessons for us today.

Black Radicalism and the Communist Party in the First Half of the Twentieth Century

> *Negroes are destined to be the most revolutionary class in America.*
> —LOVETT FORT-WHITEMAN, 1924

American black radicals never abandoned their belief that the black fight for freedom, equality, and justice was a central revolutionary struggle in its own right, even when they joined doctrinaire multiracial communist organizations. The quotation above from Lovett Fort-Whiteman, one of the very first African American members of the CPUSA, highlights an idea that was central to the identity, theory, and practice of black leftists throughout the twentieth century. The black leftists who joined multiracial leftist organizations often did so with the belief that they could carry the third path into their new Marxist organizations. To paraphrase Césaire, they believed they could make Marxism serve black liberation, as opposed to the emphasis being on how blacks could serve Marxism.

Not all black leftists agreed, of course, and eventually even Fort-Whiteman rejected his earlier views. There was yet more disagreement on how to bring the third path into the new organizations. Even brothers such as Otto Hall and Harry Haywood, two other early and extremely influential black members of the CPUSA, could bitterly disagree about how in practice one made work in support of black liberation central to the work of the organization. What the great majority of twentieth-century black leftists could agree on, despite their disagreements, was the bankruptcy of Socialist Party–type views that blacks at best had a secondary role in the movement and that the struggle for black rights was of limited importance.

Black radicalism was dominated by the CPUSA during the period from the early 1920s until 1940, with a brief postwar flurry that, not coincidentally, ended with the advent of the Cold War, just a few years before the rise of the modern civil rights movement. The party initially attracted nationalist veterans such as Harry Haywood, who were convinced that Garvey's movement was either too utopian or too opportunistic.

Haywood described why he first joined the African Blood Brotherhood and then the CPUSA but not the Garvey movement:

> We applauded some of the cultural aspects of the movement— Garvey's emphasis on race pride, dignity, self-reliance, his exultation of things Black. This was all to the good we felt. However, we rejected in its entirety the Back To Africa program as fantastic, unreal, and a dangerous diversion which could only lead to the desertion of the struggle for our rights in the USA. This was our country, we strongly felt. (Haywood 1978, 107)

Cyril Briggs, the founder of the ABB, was another early communist convert. Like many early black leftist activists, he was an immigrant from the West Indies. Like Hubert Harrison, Briggs called for the formation of a separate black nation. The ABB combined nationalism and Marxism and later became increasingly attracted to the Soviet Union. At least at first, the ABB's program was a combination of many elements, none doctrinaire Marxism.

Program of the African Blood Brotherhood Circa 1919

1. A Liberated Race
2. Absolute Race Equality
3. The Fostering of Racial Self-Respect
4. Organized and Uncompromising Opposition to the Ku Klux Klan
5. A United Negro Front
6. Industrial Development
7. Higher Wages for Negro Labor, Shorter Hours and Better Living Conditions
8. Education
9. Cooperation with Other Darker Races and the Class-Conscious White Workers (Dawson 2001, 180)

While the ABB would soon be absorbed by the CPUSA, as of 1919 its program still represented the blend of black nationalism, anticolonialism, and economic radicalism that marks the classic black synthesis of the third path. Note that the African Blood Brotherhood's program and synthetic ideology predates Du Bois and other mid-twentieth-century black radical leftists. They, along with Hubert Harrison and the Liberty League, were early pioneers in developing the third path.

Like the Liberty League, which in its "Declaration of Principles" called for "the securing of absolutely equal rights" (Perry 2009, 291), the ABB emphasized at the beginning of its program the need for both black liberation ("a liberated race") and full equality ("absolute race equality"). In Briggs's view black liberation was the only feasible alternative, especially at a time when the social democrats of the Socialist Party had abandoned their work on race and had a leadership who swore to maintain, in their own words, "white supremacy." As Solomon argues, Briggs was also deeply committed to the principle of self-determination for peoples of African descent. Like Garvey, he believed that Africans, both in Africa and throughout the diaspora, had not only the right but the duty to govern themselves (Solomon 1997). Briggs was suspicious of the Socialist Party and more generally of the social democracy of the Second International; as late as 1921 the ABB still was promoting a program that had elements of black nationalism even as the organization's leadership was moving closer to the representatives of Lenin's revolution within the United States (Solomon 1997). Eventually Briggs joined the Communist Party for reasons similar to Haywood's. As Briggs himself put it: "I entered simply because the party had a program, even [though] not written, . . . on the Negro field; because of the solution of the national question in the Soviet Union, and because I was confident that the American party in time would take its lead on that question from its Soviet party, which is what it eventually did" (Dawson 2001, 182). A significant aspect of Briggs's comment, one borne out by the historical record, is his lack of confidence in the American communists. He knew well that American socialism, whether of the Socialist Party type or the Leninist variety, was at best skeptical of how important the struggle for racial justice, let alone black liberation, would be to radical organizing in the United States. Briggs was counting on the international communist movement to force the American party to treat blacks' struggle as one with revolutionary potential in its own right.

As noted earlier, during this period some of the most savage pogroms ever launched were directed against black communities. Many blacks were extraordinarily angry—including black veterans of World War I—and were at a point at which militant action

seemed preferable to doing nothing. Blacks were also looking for
an organizational base and allies. The only two games in town for
black radicals (besides the small ABB) were the CPUSA and Garvey's UNIA. As would happen to a later generation, many of these
early and critical black Marxists eventually would be pushed out
of the organizational mainstream of the left precisely because of
their views on black liberation and the national question, and specifically their belief that the black struggle represented a revolutionary effort in its own right.

R ichard Rorty argued, "The Communist Party of the United
States (CPUSA) was of very little importance to the political life
of our country" (Rorty 1998, 44). That is certainly a plausible
argument for American politics as a whole from 1930 on, but it
does not capture the reality of black politics between the 1920s
and 1940—until the CPUSA decided to sacrifice much of its good-
will among African Americans and its hard-won gains to a Soviet-
mandated false unity that emphasized working with racist and
liberal whites who were offended by the occasionally racially
militant practices of the CPUSA. Even though black leftists were
increasingly at odds with the party over its stance toward organizing blacks, the CPUSA remained the main organizational form
that black leftists worked within during this period. While not
the only Marxist influence on black radicalism, the CPUSA did
have hegemonic organizational influence on the black left before
World War II. The third path was not followed, and the Socialist
Party (and social democrats more generally) provided little real
competition for black support even during the early years of the
CPUSA.

Communist Party work among blacks had stagnated during
the 1920s due to the CPUSA's white-dominated leadership crack-

ing down on organizing aimed at blacks. The dominant faction of the white leadership furiously opposed special status for African Americans or work among African Americans. Many in the leadership did not see the black movement as central to leftist organizing, let alone as a revolutionary movement in its own right. Black cadres argued about the best way to raise the prominence of work among blacks, with Haywood and Briggs embracing a "black nation" thesis, and others, including Haywood's brother, disagreeing. In 1922 black communists were attacked by the head of the Workers Party (the CPUSA's precursor) for protesting separate seating for black delegates to a Farmer-Labor Party convention in Chicago. Indeed, some Virginia blacks were purged for lacking the "qualifications" to be communists—they were considered too petty bourgeois, since they kept raising the question of racism within working-class organizations and meetings, and therefore were guilty of dividing the working class. It was even recommended that the entire "colored branch be dismissed" (Harris 1989, 148). As early as 1924, just as the party was taking its modern form, the main leadership faction refused to publicly demand that its members support full equality for blacks within the labor movement (Solomon 1997). Further, the Harlem branch was considered to be a den of nationalists—much the way the Socialist Party's Harlem branch had been viewed by its leadership. Not surprisingly, given this view of the black struggle and suspicion of at least some of the leading black cadres, black cadres' advice about how to organize the American Negro Labor Congress—particularly their advice that whites should not play the leading organizing role—was ignored. The result was the disaster that the black cadres had predicted, because blacks were suspicious toward whites after the great wave of antiblack pogroms that occurred between

1919 and 1923 and were understandably reluctant to join an organization dominated by whites. Finally, the dominant faction, led by Jay Lovestone, rejected organizing in the South—where the great majority of African Americans still resided—labeling the region as backward and not fit for organizing (Solomon 1997). Before 1923 there was a seemingly viable and vibrant nationalist alternative in the Universal Negro Improvement Association, but after the decline of the Garvey movement organizational options for black radicals were limited throughout much of the 1920s.

By the late 1920s, however, black cadres in Moscow working with the Communist International, the Comintern, were able to win a mandate for a resolution on a black nation. Ironically, the first version of the resolution, in 1928, was close to the formulations of many black-power-era groups such as the Black Panthers, as well as individuals such as Malcolm X. It called for support for self-determination for African Americans—the ability for blacks to be able to collectively determine their political relationship to the United States–without necessarily arguing for the existence of a black nation. The 1932 resolution was much closer to the position eventually embraced by hard-core black nationalists such as the Nation of Islam and black-power-era groups such as the Republic of New Africa, which specified a black nation based in the South.

While many cadres, including blacks, committed to black liberation scoffed at the ideal of a black nation, particularly one located in the Deep South, the mandate from Moscow did serve the intended purposes of elevating the status of organizing efforts among blacks and increasing the resources available to carry out that work. As Haywood explained:

This new line established that the Black freedom struggle is a revolutionary movement in its own right, directed against the very foundations of U.S. imperialism, with its own dynamic pace and momentum, resulting from the unfinished democratic and land revolutions in the South. It places the Black liberation movement and the class struggle of U.S. workers in their proper relationship as two aspects of the fight against the common enemy—U.S. capitalism. *It elevates the Black movement to a position of equality in that battle.* The new theory destroys forever the white racist theory traditional among class-conscious white workers which had relegated the struggle of Blacks to a subsidiary position in the revolutionary movement. (Haywood 1978, 234; emphasis added)

There was a brief flowering of successful organizing among blacks during much of the 1930s, with another brief flurry of activity in the period that followed World War II. The Communist Party during the 1930s was well received by African Americans. For example, the editor of the influential *Baltimore Afro-American* wrote, "The communists appear to be the only Party going our way" (Dawson 2001, 189). Reactionaries agreed, arguing that the Communist Party was a "black party." Just as it is dangerous for mainstream political parties today to be perceived by white Americans as the "black party," it was also dangerous for radical parties to be so perceived. Slogans such as "No jobs for niggers until every white man has a job" successfully undermined communist organizing among white workers, especially in the South, making it more difficult to build both multiracial unity and radical organizations in the South. "Black-baiting" radical parties in the South had been a successful reactionary tactic used with devastating effect to undermine southern radical organizing since the late nineteenth century (Horton 2005).

In both the North and the South strong local organizing was the foundation for building support among blacks for the CPUSA and radical politics more generally. As we saw in Chapter 1, in cities such as Chicago, organizing around housing, unemployment, and police brutality won thousands of supporters. In the South, organizing was far more clandestine, given the real threat of violence from both the state and organizations such as the Klan, but it still garnered strong support, especially from sharecroppers.[6]

Two campaigns in particular during the 1930s established the Communist Party as a national force in black politics. In the early 1930s (approximately from 1931 to 1935) the Scottsboro Boys campaign established the CPUSA's credentials in many black communities. Nine young black males falsely accused of raping two white women were sentenced to death in Alabama. Their trial and the campaign to free them, which garnered international support largely due to the communists' organizing, was extensively covered in the black press. The NAACP entered the case long after the CPUSA and its lawyers had. For its part, the Communist Party mobilized significant support nationally and internationally and brought formidable resources to the campaign. Nevertheless, both organizations contributed to saving the Scottsboro Boys, both organizations jealously fought for pride of place, and both tried to use the case to further their organization's reputation among blacks. Still, the Scottsboro campaign was a watershed event for the communists for building support within black communities. Even black cadres who were later purged for being too nationalist thought that the Scottsboro work was the Communist Party at its best, and neutral observers agreed.

By the middle 1930s, Robin Kelley argues, the Communist Party in the South had decided as part of its united-front policy to deemphasize black organizing and, as part of its plan to increase white membership, to tolerate racist behaviors that never would had been tolerated before, such as white cadres calling their black comrades "Comrade Nigger." In the North, strong organizing, particularly among black political, artistic, and intellectual elites, continued through participation in the building of a broad black united front that included diverse ideological perspectives, although the communists were the strongest organizational force. The National Negro Congress (NNC) grew out of a meeting of prominent black radicals and intellectuals at Howard University in 1935. In 1935 a "thousand fiery-eyed delegates" met in Chicago, and the NNC became one of the first—and for a brief period one of the most important—black united fronts that included a diverse sample of liberal and radical (including communist) black leaders.[7] Northern organizing fared better due to a practical focus on the economic deprivations of the Great Depression and the formation of a true united-front organization. Consequently, the National Negro Congress was able to attract black leaders—such as A. Philip Randolph, the preeminent black labor leader—who were very skeptical about communist influence in black communities, black elite intellectuals such as Ralph Bunche and E. Franklin Frazier, and other prominent leaders and intellectuals who were more open to working with communists. One reason that Randolph was more skeptical despite his grudging support for some of the party's work was that he firmly believed the U.S. party was too deferential to Moscow and would be willing to sacrifice organizing among blacks if it suited the interests of the Soviet Union. He was soon to be proven correct.

Randolph became the NNC's first president. A social democrat liberal, Randolph often clashed with the communist members of the NNC—particularly after the Nazi-Soviet alliance of 1939. Randolph also took a more nationalist perspective than communist cadres, black or otherwise, were comfortable with, arguing that "the Negro and other darker races must look to themselves for freedom" (Gilmore 2008, 310).

In many ways, however, Communist Party work within the NNC represented nearly the last hurrah of party influence within the black community. Many black radicals who had supported the antifascist efforts in Spain were disgusted by international communism's refusal to support the Ethiopians against fascist Italy's invasion or to vigorously respond to the massacre of striking dockworkers by imperial British forces in Trinidad. Black cadres were aghast as the Communist Party abandoned black-oriented work, particularly in the South. Steady purges of black cadres for nationalism began in 1936, and the Share Croppers' Union, whose black members and the black farmers they organized had suffered so much for justice, was dismantled by the national leadership of the CPUSA, which claimed it was a barrier to the "unity" of black and white workers in the South. While not as blatantly racist as the earlier Socialist Party leadership, the Communist Party leadership had decided to downplay the struggle for black equality in order to build a united front within which black interests would be subordinated domestically and internationally to the needs of the Soviet Union. By the advent of the civil rights movement, the CPUSA had squandered any remaining credibility it had in black communities.

The period between 1945 and 1955 represented a key transition for the black left in the United States. The beginning of this period saw great potential for a resurgent black left, as well as chilling portents of impending disaster. Disaster for the entire American left marked the end of this period. While state repression and the advent of the Cold War were major factors responsible for the devastation the left suffered, choices that leftists and liberals made contributed mightily as well. The result was a sundering that isolated the black left from a variety of domestic and international movements with which it had been engaged during the first half of the twentieth century. A key consequence of this sundering was that the second period of black radical insurgency would take a very different form from that of the first period. Indeed, this second insurgency would see the reemergence of the third path.

The Sundering

Between April 18 and April 24, 1955, a group Richard Wright described as "the despised, the insulted, the hurt, the dispossessed— in short, the underdogs of the human race" met in Bandung, Indonesia (Wright 1956, 12). Under the leadership of such luminaries as Jawaharlal Nehru, Zhou Enlai, and Sukarno, representatives of what would soon be erroneously but powerfully called the third world were attempting to carve out a political space for themselves in a world dominated by the Cold War. At the end of that same year, on December 5, 1955, Rosa Parks was arrested in Montgomery, Alabama, for refusing to give up her seat on a bus to a white passenger. The result of her action was the Montgomery bus boycott; this event alerted the country and the world to the growing force of the civil rights movement, which was poised to reshape

politics in the United States. Less auspicious, and much less noticed, was the final meeting of the Council on African Affairs
(CAA) on June 14, 1955. The demise of the council was one sign
among many of the decline of the black radical left that had up to
that point constituted an integral part of black politics in the
United States and throughout the black Atlantic.

As important as these three events were, not least symbolically,
jointly they represent the tip of a deeper story. In my reading,
they mark a profound sundering in black politics, particularly
black radical politics, in the United States. This small story, confined to a minority group fighting for social justice in just one
country, is more important than it would seem. I argue that this
sundering had dire consequences not only for the African American quest for justice and the emerging civil rights and later black
power movements, not only for the left in the United States but
also for the development of American politics and foreign policy.
Ultimately, this sundering led to a black liberation movement in
the 1950s, 1960s, and 1970s that was powerful and transformative
but also impoverished in a particular way. And it led to a left far
more fragmented than had been the case earlier in the twentieth
century (although this fragmentation had some positive consequences as well as many negative ones). But most important, the
sundering led to a degenerate form of politics in the United States
and the closing off of many democratic possibilities for people both
inside and outside the United States.

The decade between 1946 and 1955 saw black leftists become
marginalized within the CPUSA, the labor movement, and black
politics, largely (though not exclusively) as a result of the politics
of the deepening Cold War. These dates also mark the period in
which the civil rights movement was radically sundered from black

radicals, to the detriment of all. It is during this period that Bayard Rustin was marginalized, and Claudia Jones was arrested, imprisoned, and then deported. Paul Robeson was treated as a criminal and banned from international travel, and W. E. B. Du Bois was charged with a felony, which he beat, but he still had his passport confiscated. The fates of these more famous figures are representative of the fates of a much larger number of black leftists. It is also during this period that key organizations led by black radicals such as the National Negro Congress and the Council on African Affairs were attacked by reactionary forces and eventually forced to shut down. Pressure on these organizations was also brought to bear by the Communist Party from the left. Another key rupture occurred with the attacks by the state and other institutions on a wide range of black leftists, including Du Bois and Robeson, during the late 1940s, which isolated black leftists from their international allies. Black radical and liberal activists had been petitioning the United Nations since its formation in 1945 to investigate the United States for human rights violations with respect to African Americans. In 1947 Du Bois presented a petition to the United Nations on behalf of blacks in the United States; two years later Robeson presented another petition charging the U.S. government with genocide against African Americans. I will have more to say later about both of these petitions, as well as an earlier effort. For now, it is enough to note that as a direct result of these and other efforts to influence global politics, the state launched a ferocious counterattack that eventually suppressed black radicals' (and liberals') global initiatives. "Good Negroes" were enlisted by the State Department, media, and other institutions not only to counter the arguments of black leftists in the international arena but also to portray them as isolated, deviant, and totally out of step with grassroots blacks. By the time the Bandung meeting took place, in April 1955, the black left had already been substantially defeated by the events of the late forties and early fifties. When it reemerged in the late 1960s and early 1970s, it would be in a very different form.

During the first half of the twentieth century the black radical left was entangled with a number of other political forces and movements. Complex patterns of cooperation, and in some cases conflict, characterized relations between the black egalitarian liberal forces (found primarily in the major civil rights organizations, preeminently the NAACP), black and other radical movements outside of the United States, the labor movement, and progressive and radical forces in the United States more generally (the CPUSA being the strongest among this last group). Before World War II, black radicals and their organizations and movements were active organizing sharecroppers, defending the Scottsboro Boys, and building broad united-front organizations that included many of the leading black activists and intellectuals as well as organizations such the National Negro Congress (Gilmore 2008). By the closing days of World War II, black radicals such as Du Bois were working with the NAACP to try to influence the creation and implementation of the newly formulated United Nations Declaration on Human Rights (Anderson 2003; Von Eschen 1997). Throughout the first half of the century, black radicals from the United States participated in key events and movements in alliance with a wide range of forces inside the country, and they were represented and active at international conferences convened to fight colonialism, examine the plight of peoples of African descent, and contribute to the worldwide struggle for human rights. Despite tensions and setbacks—many self-inflicted (to be discussed later)—in the late

1930s and during the war, by 1945 black radicalism was poised once again to be a major player in progressive movements nationally and internationally.

Yet a decade later, with two defining moments of the anticolonial and civil rights movement taking place in Bandung and Montgomery, respectively, black radicalism and black radicals were not a factor. Explaining the importance of Bandung, Indonesia's Sukarno spoke for many:

> For many generations our peoples have been the voiceless ones in the world. We have been the unregarded, the peoples for whom decisions were made by others whose interests were paramount, the peoples who lived in poverty and humiliation. . . . What can we do? The peoples of Asia and Africa wield little physical power. Even our economic strength is dispersed and slight. We cannot indulge in power politics. . . . Our statesmen, by and large, are not backed up with serried ranks of jet bombers. . . . We, the peoples of Asia and Africa, 1,400,000,000 strong, far more than half of the population of the world, we can mobilize what I have called the Moral Violence of Nations in favor of peace. (Wright 1956, 139)

Delegates to the conference also explicitly linked the struggle against colonialism and exploitation to the struggle for racial equality. As one Philippine cabinet member put it:

> I have said that besides the issues of colonialism and political freedom, all of us here are concerned with the matter of racial equality. This is a touchstone, I think, for most of us assembled here are the people we represent. The systems and the

manners of it have varied, but there has not been and there is not a Western colonial regime which has not imposed, to a greater or lesser degree, on the people it ruled the doctrine of their own racial inferiority. (Wright 1956, 151)

The main African American presence at Bandung, however, was Harlem's representative to Congress, Adam Clayton Powell Jr., whose main role was to attack communism whether in the Soviet Union, China, or Vietnam, to discredit African American leftists such as Du Bois and Robeson, and to paint a crudely false and rosy picture of the status of blacks in the United States (Anderson 2003; Von Eschen 1997). The State Department explicitly tried to limit African American participation at Bandung, even for its allies such as Powell (Anderson 2003; Von Eschen 1997). Thus African American presence at this critical international forum was largely nonexistent—a radical departure from even a decade earlier, when black radicals and liberals were a constant, active presence on the world stage.

Equally noticeable was the lack of a black radical presence in Montgomery and the early civil rights movement more generally. Whether in the quest for jobs and fair housing in the North or in organizing for equal rights and the end of Jim Crow in the South, black radicals had been an integral part of the struggle for civil rights earlier in the twentieth century—often, although certainly not always, taking a leading role (Anderson 2003; Biondi 2003; Gilmore 2008). By the mid-1950s, the older and more established civil rights organizations, and particularly the NAACP's leadership, were actively opposed to communism, leftism, and internationalism. While it would become clear that newer organizations such as King's Southern Christian Leadership Council (SCLC) and the mostly student-based Student Nonviolent Coordinating Committee (SNCC) would prove to be open to radical ideas, black radical presence in the early civil rights movement at both the organizational and social movement levels was nonexistent.

By 1955 black radicalism had been brutally and efficiently sundered from all of the movements with which it had been entangled domestically and internationally. One result was that in many cases the black movement as a whole was isolated from these other movements, as black radicals had been the ones playing the primary bridging role. By "isolated" I do not mean that, at least in some cases, there was not awareness of and support for these other movements. For example, in 1956 King was clearly linking the Montgomery movement to the nonaligned movement and a romanticized Bandung when he argued:

> Now I am aware of the fact that there are those who would contend that we live in the most ghastly period of human history. They would argue that the rhythmic beat of the deep rumblings of discontent from Asia, the uprisings in Africa, the nationalistic longings of Egypt, the roaring cannons from Hungary, and the racial tensions of America are all indicative of the deep and tragic midnight which encompasses our civilization. They would argue that we are retrogressing instead of progressing. But far from presenting retrogression and tragic meaninglessness, the present tensions represent the necessary pains that accompany the birth of anything new. . . . Whenever there is the emergence of the new we confront the recalcitrance of the old. So the tensions which we witness in the world today are indicative of the facts that a new world order is being born, and an old order is passing away. (King 1986b, 135)

In April 1957 he continued this line of attack in another speech, this time naming Bandung directly:

> We are not fighting for ourselves alone, but we are fighting for this nation. *(Amen, Yes)* Go back and tell those people who are telling us to slow up that there are approximately two billion four hundred million people in this world. Go back and tell them that two-thirds of these people are colored. *(Yes sir)* Go back and tell them that one billion six hundred million of the people of the world are colored. *(Yes)* Most of them live on two continents. Six hundred million in China. Four hundred million in India and Pakistan. A hundred million in Indonesia. Two hundred million in Africa. Eighty-six million in Japan. These people for years have lived under the bondage of colonialism and imperialism. *(Yes sir)* One day they got tired. *(Go ahead)* One day these people got tired of being trampled over by the iron feet of oppression. *(Yes, Go ahead)* One day they got tired of being pushed out of the glittering sunlight of life's July and left standing in the piercing chill of an Alpine November. *(Look out, Look out)* So as a result of their tiredness they decided to rise up and protest against colonialism and imperialism. As a result of their rising up, more than one billion three hundred million of the colored peoples of the world have broken a-loose from colonialism and imperialism. *(Yes sir)* They have broken a-loose from the Egypt of colonialism. [*applause*] *(Go ahead)* They have broken a-loose from the Egypt of colonialism, and now they are moving through the wilderness of adjustment toward the promised land of cultural integration. And as they look back you know what they are saying? "Racism and colonialism must go in

this world." *(Yes)* They assembled in Bandung some months ago, and that was the word that echoed from Bandung *(Yes):* "Racism and colonialism must go." (King 2000, 175–176)

The black press also took notice of Bandung. The *Baltimore Afro-American* called Bandung "a turning point in world history," one in which "the majority of the world's people think there is an alternative to following blindly the lead of either Russia or the United States" (Von Eschen 1997, 168). The black press also noted Powell's presence. One black journalist stated that Powell had sold colored people down the river.

Despite the intense attacks on black radicalism, vestiges of an internationalist consciousness linking anticolonial struggles abroad to the struggle against racism at home continued to exist. What had been sundered were the political and organizational ties to the networks that had allowed black radicals to operate on many fronts, to bring allies to the black quest for social justice, and to connect the struggle to other progressive movements domestically and internationally. The results of the sundering included a narrowing of focus in the black movement for several years, a rightward trend in American politics that continues to this day, and, just as important, the diminution of the capacity for activists and Americans more generally to imagine and build a more democratic politics and polity. Periods of democratic mobilization and progressive public policy innovation within the United States, such as those that occurred during Reconstruction, the populist insurgency of the late nineteenth century, the New Deal, and the Great Society, have been associated with high levels of black mobilization and interracial alliances. The sundering, as we will see, led to fragmentation and disarticulation of these movements and alliances, and American politics never fully recovered.

Entanglement

The concept of "entanglement" that I am using to describe black radicalism during the middle of the twentieth century entails more than simple interconnection among black radicals, their organizations, their movements, and a variety of other movements and political forces. Instead, I am using "entanglement" in a sense borrowed from quantum mechanics, which allows it to serve as a rich and suitable metaphor for analyzing mid-twentieth-century black radicalism. In 1947, in the second edition of his tome *The Principles of Quantum Mechanics,* Paul Dirac described the concept of superposition at the center of entanglement as follows:

> The general principle of superposition of quantum mechanics applies to the states [that are theoretically possible without mutual interference or contradiction]. . . . of any one dynamical system. It requires us to assume that between these states there exist peculiar relationships such that whenever the system is definitely in one state we can consider it as being partly in each of two or more other states. The original state must be regarded as the result of a kind of superposition of the two or more new states, in a way that cannot be conceived on classical ideas. (Dirac 1947, 12)

I contend that as long as black radicalism was entangled with numerous other social and political forces, any given political moment contained a number of different futures (or states). While each of these movements and political forces was a separate entity to some degree, they affected each other in ways that were not predictable. Further, by having these separate movements articulated with black radical movements, there existed many different potential democratic futures that were more unrealizable and, just as important, unimaginable if black radicalism became isolated. An effect of the sundering was to collapse these futures, as political cooperation between multiple movements ended and democratic futures faded from the imagination and were assigned to the realm of the "impossible." The separation of the labor movement from black radical movements, for example, made the macroeconomic goal of government-guaranteed full employment increasingly unimaginable after the late 1940s. Possible futures disappeared as American politics collapsed into a degenerate state in which the lack of alignment among movements was a blow to the struggles for black liberation, civil rights, human rights, and progressive internationalism in the United States.

Circa 1948 the key entanglements of black radical movements in the United States were with the civil rights movement; the labor movement, particularly the Congress of Industrial Organizations (CIO); political movements of the black Atlantic, particularly anticolonial movements; and a sprinkling of other international radical movements. Each entanglement had its own tensions, contradictions, and possibilities, both individually and in combination with others. Playing the role of bridges within and across entanglements were a number of individual black radicals. For example, Bayard Rustin provided links between the civil rights, labor, pacifist, and black radical movements. W. E. B. Du Bois moved between black radical, civil rights, black Atlantic, and international movements. Claudia Jones bridged black radical, women's, and black Atlantic movements, and Paul Robeson the international, civil rights, black radical, arts, and labor movements. A key mechanism of the sundering was to remove these bridging figures through prosecution, persecution, and marginalization (Kelley 2002). Also important were organizations such as the NNC domestically and the CAA in the international arena, which provided critical bridges between different political forces and movements. The removal of these bridging black radicals and their organizations from domestic and international politics was a critical step in destroying relationships that were essential to the foundation of multiple democratic possibilities.

In U.S. black radical history there have been a number of key moments of potential with multiple states/futures existing simultaneously. These moments can be characterized as occurring when black civil society is strong, when multiple black political tendencies are active, and when these black political movements have strong and complex ties with multiple social and political forces outside the black community. The black political movements in question tend to be leftist, but they are sometimes black nationalist, radical, or liberal. The years between approximately 1910 and 1919 were one such period. The years between 1945 and 1950 were another. During these periods a series of events in combination with choices black political actors made led to identifiable patterns of radical politics that held for a number of years or even decades and defined an era. After World War I the pattern that emerged dominated black radical politics until the end of World War II. The pattern that emerged after 1948 lasted only ten to fifteen years but arguably had a more devastating effect on black, progressive, and American politics.

It is important to understand the role contingency and agency had in shaping the future. Retrospectively, to some historians the sundering has appeared inevitable. For example, Penny Von Eschen refers to "the liberal and left coalitions of the 1940s that had become impossible during the Cold War" (Von Eschen 1977, 170). Impossible? Does she mean that they were impossible to imagine or that they were impossible in fact? Certainly the American government used its entire repressive coercive power to destroy the left and its connection to any other movement or social force. Yet it is the role of the political imagination to imagine what seems impossible. And it is not clear to me that liberal left coalitions were impossible in fact during the early Cold War in or outside of the black movement. Later in the Cold War, during the next surge of black radicalism in the late 1960s and 1970s, the full power of the state was once again turned on black radicalism in both its leftist and nationalist forms. In some ways these attacks were even more violent than those that occurred during the Red Scare of the late forties and fifties. There were outright police assassinations of leaders, such as the Black Panther Party's Fred Hampton in Chicago in December 1969. Black nationalists, leftists, and others were targeted for killing, imprisonment, or harassment, as were the organizations to which they belonged. Numerous trials, including many famous ones involving the Black Panther Party, could have eventually led to death sentences, and many did lead to long prison terms.

As in the earlier period, black liberals and leftists often were antagonistic to each other. Yet, generally, elements of the black liberal community and the black grass roots did not turn on black radicals as they had during the period after 1948. When black radicals became isolated this time, it was due as much to their own political choices as to state repression and internecine fighting. Coalitions between leftists and liberals can be difficult to sustain in any period, but in each period political actors' choices have played a different role in determining the fate of the coalitions. Massive state pressures were brought to bear on black radicalism in both periods, but the choices of movement actors (both radical and liberal) also led to black radical movements' eventual demise in both periods. In the next section I examine key choices that enabled the sundering.

Sundering

By the late 1930s, African American activists were angry. They were angry about the continued level of lethal violence, particularly the brutal lynchings directed toward black citizens both in and outside the Jim Crow South. Blacks were feeling betrayed by the Roosevelt administration, which had done precious little toward advancing racial equality in the United States. Black radical liberal A. Philip Randolph proclaimed, "American democracy is a failure. It is a miserable failure" (Anderson 2003, 8).[8] Many black activists were disturbed by, and opposed to, the CPUSA's united-front policy, which seemed to call for a partial withdrawal from work for black liberation. Furthermore, as noted earlier in this chapter, they were also upset with the Soviet Union for its refusal to treat the Italian fascists' invasion of Ethiopia with the kind of militancy international communism had shown backing the Republican forces in Spain during their battle with international and domestic fascism. As Foner argued, "It was to be exceedingly difficult for the communists to overcome the resentment among blacks created by the Party's wartime policies. The communists never completely erased the feelings in sections of the black community that they placed the Soviet Union's survival above the battle for black equality" (Marable 2007, 19).

As World War II approached, black activists and elites focused on three themes in particular. One was a call to desegregate the armed forces. A second was to desegregate defense industries receiving federal dollars. Third was the so-called Double V campaign, which was embraced by a very wide spectrum of African Americans. The Double V campaign called for victory against fascism internationally and victory against racism at home. Some in government viewed this campaign as treasonous, a stance that recalled the government's view of black agitation for racial equality during World War I. Nevertheless, throughout the war black civil rights and other liberal forces pursued the Double V campaign in fighting for the end of Jim Crow in the workplace, the military, and civil society. Black radicals also supported the campaign, including those in the leftist-led Negro National Congress, which had strong ties to the CPUSA. The NNC decided to support Double V both out of conviction about its righteousness and because of the realization that not to do so would entail forfeiting substantial credibility in the black community (Anderson 2003). The CPUSA had previously denounced the campaign, and NNC's support generated wrath and led the party to rethink its support for the black organization (Anderson 2003). The campaign won some victories, but more important was that by the end of the war a tone of militancy had become well established in black politics.

The Soviet alliance with the Nazis at the beginning of World War II spelled doom for the National Negro Congress and the black united front, which up till then had been very successful. Black activists outside the direct influence of the Communist Party righteously remained antifascist and, following the lead of A. Philip Randolph and others, rejected out of hand the abandonment of the antifascist line forced on the NNC by the CPUSA and its sympathizers. The damage had been permanently done despite the Soviet embrace of the antifascist alliance in the summer of 1941 after the Nazi invasion of the Soviet Union during Operation Barbarossa. Many black cadres and supporters would never forgive the party for its betrayal of its antifascist principles and for its slavish adherence to the Soviet line. Bayard Rustin, for example, broke with the CPUSA in June 1941 due to the party's hostility toward work among blacks such as the Double V campaign (D'Emilio 2003). As one party member remarked about Harlem, "The Party began to lose its 'base' and the foundations of Popular Front organizations began to crumble" (Gilmore 2008, 306).

The relationship between black liberals and their organizations, on one hand, and black leftists and theirs, on the other, remained rocky throughout this period, but cooperation continued on specific campaigns and in the context of united-front organizations with members from both factions, such as the NNC and the CAA. Black liberals, particularly civil rights leaders such as Roy Wilkins and Walter White, remained suspicious of both organizations because of the active participation of Communist Party cadres. Nevertheless, black radical liberals such as Randolph, Bunche, and White (the last of these in his capacity as leader of the NAACP) continued to work with the black left. Some, preeminently W. E. B. Du Bois, had roots in both camps—a position that could be maintained only with great difficulty and which became increasingly untenable. However, the fact that "Communists and various Socialists were ubiquitous in civil rights battles during the 1940s" ensured that during much of the decade a united front between black leftists and liberals persisted (Sugrue 2008, 103).

Despite increasing tension between the black left and liberal factions, representatives from thirty-four organizations, including the NAACP, met in June 1945 to forge a new strategy—one aimed at shaping the United Nations' human rights initiative in a way that would explicitly tie the fight for human rights to anticolonial struggles. The participants clearly saw the fight against racial inequality and violence in the United States as linked to the anticolonial struggles breaking out throughout what would become known as the third world. As Mary McLeod Bethune, one of the century's leading black liberals, put it, the "Negro in America [held] little more than colonial status in a democracy" (Anderson 2003, 57).

The momentum from the June 1945 meeting would carry over into 1946 and 1947, receiving a powerful grassroots boost as black veterans of World War II returned home and started organizing for racial democracy with a vengeance. In southern states such as Georgia and North Carolina during 1946 and 1947 black veterans organized "regiments" to register blacks to vote. In Charlotte, North Carolina, a black funeral home owner founded the Citizens Committee for Political Action to "promote the political, social and economic welfare" (Gilmore 2008, 415). The organization undertook political education, invited outside speakers, promoted black candidates, and generally engaged in political action and mobilization. By 1950 the group had registered several thousand new black voters. These efforts were aided by the CIO's Political Action Committee (CIO-PAC). CIO-PAC hired a veteran black leftist, Henry Lee Moon, as an organizer. Moon had become disenchanted with Stalin and the CPUSA's pullback of support for black liberation in the United States. Under his leadership the labor organization began a massive black voter registration campaign in the South. They told white workers and their allies in the South that they were interested in registering black voters not in order to achieve "social equality" (southern code for integration—especially miscegenation—and anathema to most white southerners) but to achieve economic equality for the South within the nation. Black voters, white workers were told, would greatly aid in achieving that aim (Gilmore 2008).

On the international front, the NAACP (particularly under the leadership of Du Bois) and the NNC both tried to influence the UN stand on human rights. They encountered massive resistance from the U.S. government, especially from Eleanor Roosevelt, a key member of the U.S. delegation, who saw as her main role preventing the UN from hearing petitions charging the United States with human rights violations with respect to blacks. She used her position on the NAACP board to pressure the organization to back off the idea of petitioning the UN, and she pointedly instructed the organization to rein in Du Bois, who had by far the most militant position on human rights among those in the leadership. The NNC took the lead in presenting "A Petition to the United Nations on Behalf of 13 Million Oppressed Negro Citizens of the United States of America" to the United Nations on June 6, 1946. After the UN demanded proof of the charges, the NNC mounted a campaign designed to gather such proof (Anderson 2003).

In 1946 there were also signs of the trouble to come. The NNC itself was on its last legs, as the CPUSA had started to pull its support when the NNC leadership resisted the party's push for tighter control. The Red Scare was intensifying, depriving the NNC of material and political support as sources of funding dried up and allies disappeared (Anderson 2003; Gilmore 2008). By 1947 the

NNC would no longer be a functioning organization. The year 1946 also saw an antiblack backlash in the South. No sooner had black veterans arrived home than they began to be targeted for murder, to keep both them and blacks more generally in their place. These attacks in the South were explicitly supported and in some cases planned by those in the highest offices to enforce white supremacy (Anderson 2003). The Red Scare quickly followed. North Carolina labor leaders openly attacked anyone vaguely affiliated with the Communist Party. By 1947, black ministers in states such as North Carolina were also attacking the CPUSA's program for black progress (Gilmore 2008).

After World War II communists once again organized for black rights in the North. Many of these struggles included participation in antidiscrimination work in cities such as New York. Once again blacks were facing an alliance of powerful corporations, white civic associations, the state, and all too often elements of the white labor movement, all working together to preserve white privilege in the form of exclusive access to labor, real estate, and consumer markets as well as public goods such as parks and beaches (well into the 1970s blacks often used such recreation areas at risk of their own lives). Real estate practices in New York provide just one example of the monumental lengths that the state and corporate America were willing to go to codify and enforce the racial order in the North. In the late 1940s civil rights organizers, including communist organizers, had to face an alliance of the large insurance company Met Life and power broker Robert Moses (the unelected czar of building and public authorities in metropolitan New York from the 1930s through much of the 1960s) when trying to desegregate the Stuyvesant Town housing development. This corporate–political alliance was backed by the police and local media such as the *New York Times* and *New York Herald-Tribune* (Biondi 2003). Where legal codes, corporate practices, and social pressure didn't work, the last resort was violence aimed at blacks seeking better housing. Violence has always been the ultimate tool for enforcing the racial order. Black women played a key role both in "bearing witness" and in mobilizing an antiviolence crusade in both North and South. Civil rights organizing throughout the country, including the attempt to desegregate Stuyvesant Town, was constantly attacked as being a communist plot.

The initial signs of the sundering could be perceived as early as 1947, even while the black left-liberal coalition was still operating in some domains at a high level. The NAACP stepped in where the NNC had left off, presenting its own extremely well-documented petition to the UN. On October 23, 1947, under public pressure orchestrated to a significant degree by Du Bois (outraging NAACP leadership, particularly Walter White), the UN accepted the NAACP's petition. Titled "An Appeal to the World: A Statement on the Denial of Human Rights to Minorities in the Case of Citizens of Negro Descent in the United States of America and an Appeal to the United Nations for Redress," the petition received extremely strong support in the black media and the black public sphere (Anderson 2003). It was received with the utmost hostility by the social forces ruling the South, as well as by those who supported white supremacy and/or did not want to antagonize racist southern political leaders, particularly the southern Democrats.

Indeed, the NAACP's growing dependence on and deference to Truman's Democratic Party, masterminded by Walter White, Roy Wilkins, and their allies, would be responsible for a key element of the sundering, entailing the full repudiation of a militant program supporting an international strategy to win racial equality, an attack on the black left, and a narrowing of the entire agenda to one of incremental, gradual change conducted mostly through the courts. First, the NAACP immediately began to tone down support for its own petition to the UN, assuring the State Department that it would not allow itself to be used as a wedge in a way that ran counter to U.S. Cold War policy.

The pivotal year for the NAACP was 1948. Over the course of that year the NAACP withdrew all support for the petition, stating that in submitting it the organization had merely been appeasing Du Bois's whims. More decisively, at nearly the same time, in September 1948, the board of the NAACP fired Du Bois. Tensions had been building for years. The official charge was that Du Bois supported Henry Wallace rather than Truman in the presidential campaign under way at the time. The NAACP leadership went on to violate its own rules barring support for any candidate by openly supporting Truman and in effect becoming the Truman campaign's most effective instrument in the black community. The membership and local leadership went into shock over Du Bois's dismissal, and many condemned the decision. One local leader argued that the firing meant the full endorsement of U.S. foreign policy, which in turn meant endorsing the "enslavement and imperialistic exploitation of colonial peoples" (Anderson 2003, 145). In this sentiment he was not alone.

The first period comes to an end with the terror of the anticommunist repression. As the crusade against communism intensified, black and white liberals, the organized labor movement, and some black nationalists all strove to distance themselves not only from the Communist Party but also from radical politics more generally, abandoning tactics such as mobilizing grassroots protest. The Red Scare was now in full swing, and black leftists were under immense pressure from the state and from black liberals in and outside the NAACP who actively collaborated in attacks on Robeson, Du Bois, and others. One vice president of the organization, a judge named Jane Bolin, was aghast and resigned because she now believed the leadership was conducting a witch hunt and was no longer concerned with fighting for racial equality for blacks (Anderson 2003, 167).

Despite protests by some national board members, the NAACP went on to engage in an extraordinary retreat that bordered on self-destruction. As reasons for its abandonment of mass black struggle, the NAACP cited not only alleged left-wing involvement but anti-black-nationalist reasons as well (Biondi 2003; Marable 2007; Sugrue 2008). For example, the reason it offered for not supporting a black dockworkers union fighting Jim Crow union practices in New York was the union's "all-black identity and association with the left" (Biondi 2003, 254). Many local NAACP branches were permanently crippled. Just in the New York metropolitan area, the powerful Brooklyn branch as well as branches in Flushing, Corona, Jamaica, Great Neck, and Freeport were systematically "purged," to use Biondi's apt language, of radical elements and elements that opposed the new anticommunist drive even though only eight branches nationwide were thought to be targets of communist infiltration (Biondi 2003, 167–169). Beginning in 1948 the Congress of Racial Equality (CORE) joined the NAACP in purging leftist elements within its chapters even though only a few chapters had Marxist members (Marable 2007). The result of the anticommunist drive within the civil rights movement, according to one astute and veteran activist, Ewart Guinier, was that "the direction of them [the Urban League and NAACP], was taken over by whites, whites who were afraid of Blacks that they considered radical" (Biondi 2003, 171).

Black nationalists in New York also cooperated with diverse anticommunist movements in attacking veteran black leftist leaders, such as the oft-elected black communist Benjamin Davis—an ironic reversal from a quarter century earlier, when leftist and liberal forces cooperated with the state to bring down Marcus Garvey. During the same period as the black nationalist attack on Davis, major black liberals such as Randolph, Wilkins, and Powell cooperated with the state in suppressing "one of the most famous and admired Americans in the world"—Paul Robeson (Biondi 2003, 155). The incidents in both the 1920s and 1950s—both periods of active oppression aimed at black movements—marked disgraceful behavior on the part of those who cooperated with the state and other racist forces to suppress rival wings of the black movement. Marable estimates that the black movement was set back a decade by the cooperation of the NAACP's White and others with the state's campaign to smash the black left (Marable 2007, 31). Black leftists could find few resources anywhere to continue the fight for racial equality.

The attack on the black left was not limited to persecution of individuals such as Du Bois, Jones, and Robeson, or organizations such as the NNC and CAA. It was also an attack against the ideas of black radicalism. For example, despite Du Bois's acquittal, his "voluminous writings on Negro sociology, history and politics were removed from thousands of libraries and universities" (Marable 2007, 26).

Some continued to try. Communist William Patterson, secretary of the Civil Rights Congress (in some ways a successor organization to the NNC), wrote his own petition to the United Nations. "We Charge Genocide," released in February 1951, was a worry for the State Department because it was recognized as an extremely well-crafted petition, based on some of the State Department's own documents, in addition to others from the NAACP. White, at the head of the NAACP, was only too eager to take up the challenge of discrediting Patterson and the petition. Other members of the leadership once again attacked White and his collaborators for doing the State Department's bidding. It was noted that the document they were attacking made essentially the same charges the NAACP had advanced just a few years earlier (Anderson 2003). Patterson's lack of a clear plan on how to use the petition also contributed to its demise, however. He was trying to use it to rally support in the black community for communists under attack by the state.

The campaign to suppress "We Charge Genocide" was succeeding when events in Florida intervened. Throughout this period there had been murderous attacks aimed at Jewish, Catholic, and black citizens—including the official murder of unarmed young black prisoners by a Florida sheriff. None of these brutal crimes had been prosecuted. The head of the state NAACP, Harry T. Moore, had had enough. He publicly enjoined the state to defend black people and the Constitution of the United States. The response was a bomb that blew apart his house on Christmas night in 1951, killing him and his wife, Harriette (Anderson 2003; Biondi 2003). The outrage in the black community was monumental, and the NAACP's description of a United States in which steady progress was being made was seen as brutally absurd. Nevertheless, the United States was able to prevent debate of Patterson's petition at the UN. With the collaboration of the other Western powers and to some degree the Soviet Union and its allies, UN policy on human rights was crafted to ensure that cases such as that of African Americans would be considered purely "internal" matters outside the purview of the UN.

The NAACP shifted to the right in the domestic sphere as well. As we have seen, in 1948 the organization demanded partisan purity (support for Truman's Democratic Party) and used it as a pretext to purge Du Bois. In 1950 Roy Wilkins engineered an ideological purity test, winning a resolution that required the organization "to take the necessary action to suspend and reorganize, or lift the charter and expel any branch . . . coming under Communist . . . domination" (Biondi 2003, 167). According to Biondi, the result was the dismantling of activist NAACP branches through the United States and a full demobilization of the organization by 1952 (Biondi 2003).

By 1953 the sundering was complete. Biondi describes one consequence of it, writing that "capital and labor in the United States reached a rapprochement" (Biondi 2003, 250). This rapprochement was terrible news for black activists. Labor, which had been an ally, albeit an unreliable one, would from now on be frequently allied with forces hostile to black aspirations for equality and justice. By the mid-1950s, liberal stalwarts such as Bunche and Randolph who had been complicit in the purges were themselves charged by the government with disloyalty. Bunche was able to beat the charges, but the case remains a clear example of what can come of backing a government intent on dismantling black radicalism in all of its forms. During the same period the State Department took NAACP material off its approved lists. It was not just the state that now launched an attack on their former black liberal allies. A 1959 attempt by black labor to organize led the AFL-CIO to label the esteemed labor leader Randolph and the other organizers "racists" for daring to fight for the equality of black workers (Biondi 2003, 282–283); Randolph was formally censured by the AFL-CIO.

Of course, the purges of the left were not confined to the civil rights movement. The CIO was conducting similar purges of its own. And the black left had other problems that were connected to government repression. The fact that the labor "movement," which had ceased being a mass movement and was becoming increasingly dominated by right-wing, racist bureaucrats, was now part of the problem and not the solution was a critical difference between the beginning and end of the first period, and a difference that made black radicalism's task much more difficult going forward. This separation between black and labor movements contributed in turn to more nationalist-inflected versions of black radicalism, as was also the case in the first two decades of the twentieth century. What Biondi correctly describes as a "rapprochement" between (white) labor and capital in the United States was part of a phenomenon, Eley argues, that occurred throughout the West—a rapprochement that used the super-profits generated by colonies and the U.S. domestic nonwhite populations to buy labor "peace" with the privileged, predominantly white U.S. and European working classes (Biondi 2003; Eley 2007).

The CPUSA, which was being threatened by extinction, increasingly withdrew from work on racial equality in favor of trying to maintain its existence. The collapse and isolation of the black radical left was also strongly a result of the CPUSA's own policies. The party shut down entire branches and withdrew from active organizing in many spheres as a direct result of the Red Scare and the McCarthyite attack on communists and their sympathizers.

Just as damaging, as early as 1953 major party theorists such as James Jackson were arguing that the struggle for black rights was no longer a revolutionary struggle in its own right and that indeed the "Negro" was well on his way to full economic and political assimilation. As a result of this change in policy, the CPUSA backed the NAACP's strategies and saw any hint of nationalism as reactionary (Biondi 2003; Haywood 1978).

Yet despite the "full assimilation" predicted by leading Communist Party theorists, a 1963 survey demonstrated that racial discrimination still was an overwhelming force shaping black lives: "in Los Angeles, Boston, Chicago, and Philadelphia . . . 90 to 97 percent of employment agencies were willing to engage in overt racial discrimination," and a similar pattern was found in New York (Biondi 2003, 269). As the dramatic eruption of the mass civil rights movement demonstrated, despite the Pollyannaish predictions of communist theorists, conditions were ripe for a militant new phase of mass black insurgency. By the long hot summers—the urban disturbances—of the middle 1960s it was also clear that the northern and western ghettos were smoldering seedbeds for a new wave of black radicalism—a wave that would follow the third path, which had been largely abandoned in the early 1920s.

The implications of the sundering were apparent in particular in the absence of black radicals in 1955 from both Bandung and Montgomery. Their absence offered radical proof of how a new equilibrium had come from the devastation caused by the collapse of the previously entangled forces and superposed states—the entanglement of black radical politics with black liberalism, labor, and the international progressive and anticolonial movements (Anderson 2003). It was also in 1955 that the CAA finally collapsed. Ironically, the CAA's last breath was used to portray Bandung as

proof of the validity of its approach to foreign policy and anticolonial struggles, as well as the necessity for left–liberal alliances (Von
Eschen 1997). By Bandung and Montgomery the political work
of the sundering was largely complete, although the repression
would continue for several years.

Consequences

One of the key factors in the success of the sundering was the
overly close, often slavish ties between black radical liberals and
the Democratic Party, which would eventually lead some of them
to be active collaborators during the Red Scare and the attack on
the black left. Ironically, if predictably, black radical liberals such as
Bunche, Randolph, and the NAACP leadership themselves became
the targets of the McCarthyites once their services in attacking the
black left were no longer needed. On the other hand, black leftists were tied too closely, often also slavishly, to the CPUSA and
ultimately Moscow, which frequently led them to collaborate in
the dismantling of work in the black liberation movement and
independent black organizations and to downplay the struggle for
racial justice. The black left was compromised in this way during
the united-front period in the late 1930s, during World War II
when the CPUSA refused to support the black Double V campaign against fascism overseas and racism at home, and again with
the intensification of the Red Scare and the sacrifice of work for
racial equality in favor of efforts to merely survive the state's
attack. It is understandable that activists in the black freedom
struggle needed and sought powerful allies, but both liberals and
leftists ended up elevating the needs of those outside forces over
the needs of the freedom struggle. These alliances with strong
political forces outside the black community, forces that at best

considered the struggle for black liberation to be a low priority and all too often were hostile to it, contributed to the estrangement of radical liberals and leftists alike, and severely damaged the movement as a whole.

A key consequence of the sundering was that when the black liberation movement took off again, with Chicano, Puerto Rican, Native American, Asian American, and Hawaiian movements also exploding onto the national scene, the language it adopted was not that of the period before the sundering—the language of working-class struggle and the struggle for racial equality. Instead, the pre-eminent language was that of national liberation and anticolonial struggles. This was most starkly the case for the Puerto Rican, Hawaiian, and Native American movements, but it was true for nationalist and many leftist elements of the other movements as well. Nearly two decades before Jesse Jackson built his Rainbow Coalition to support his presidential campaigns of 1984 and 1988, groups within these movements had already embraced a strategy of coming together first in coalitions and then perhaps at some point in broader, multiracial organizations. Even when the new communist movement itself was calling for broader multiracial organizations, its language was telling. Instead of "multiracial alliances," the preferred phrasing was "multinational alliances," once again denoting the unity of various "national movements."[9] Indeed, this is how the majority of these organizations had formed—at least those with any significant number of cadres of color. These new communist organizations often developed out of the merger between black, Chicano, Puerto Rican, and Asian American leftist organizations. A related consequence of the sundering between black liberals and the left is that during the black power era black leftists ended up more frequently in coalitions with black nationalists than with black liberals, unlike the way alliances were made in the previous period.

Among the most damaging consequences of the sundering was the severe estrangement it occasioned between African American and white workers, so that by the time the black radical movement in the United States rebuilt in the mid- to late 1960s, the two groups of workers all too often viewed each other as enemies. In this period, white racial resentment was consciously manipulated first by George Wallace; then came Richard Nixon and his handlers, who in the late 1960s forged a reactionary populist bastion in the South that is still with us today, not least at the grass roots of the Tea Party. When black radicals got involved in labor organizing in the sixties in the San Francisco Bay Area, in Mahwah, New Jersey, in New York City, and most dramatically in Detroit, they faced extreme difficulty winning over rank-and-file white workers. Frequently, as in Detroit, they had to fight the unions, which had allied themselves with capital and forces of racial reaction.[10] Neither black nor white leftists of the time had a sufficiently developed analysis of the structural changes occurring in American capitalism as one of the causes, if a mostly invisible one, of the conflict between black and white workers. Without such an analysis, the process of winning white workers to the battle against white supremacy was poorly understood and proved difficult to achieve.

A third consequence of the sundering was an unfortunate twist taken by black leftist internationalism. Black activists had been present at Versailles after World War I and in San Francisco in 1945, and indeed at most of the major international conferences between 1918 and 1945. African American activists had gained firsthand experience with the Soviets from the 1920s through the

1940s. Consequently, they had few illusions about the nature of either the Western powers or the Soviets and their allies. Not being at Bandung or at the major events on the world stage for most of the 1950s meant that the new black activists had few ties with the third world as it emerged at the meeting, and except for a few individuals, such as Richard Wright, blacks from the United States did not witness the strategic maneuvers being undertaken by the likes of Nehru and Zhou on behalf of their own states' interests (Kelly 2012). Thus many of the young activists of the 1960s had a romanticized view of the national liberation movements and newly independent countries of the third world.

What was also sundered for the vast majority of those in the black liberation movement were ties to the Communist Party of the Soviet Union, ties that already had been severely damaged by policies issuing from Moscow during the late 1930s and 1940s. Unfortunately, one lesson from the previous period had not been learned. Starting with the Panthers, a significant segment of black radicals in the late 1960s and early 1970s embraced, largely uncritically, another foreign communist state, China, as did many Latino, Asian, and white radicals and communists. This embrace entailed uncritical acceptance of the Cultural Revolution and, disastrously for building relationships with progressive forces in Africa, liberation movements in southern Africa that neither had popular support nor were particularly radical or transformative, their only virtue being that they were the faction that China supported in opposition to the faction supported by the Soviet Union (such as the Pan African Congress in South Africa instead of the African National Congress).

Yet another consequence of the sundering was the relative loss of intergenerational continuity between black leftists of the 1930s and 1940s and the new generation of black-power-era leftists, especially when compared to their black nationalist and liberal contemporaries. Both the repression against the left (not just the left tied to the CPUSA) and the rejection of the CPUSA's approach to black struggle by most black activists meant that black leftists in many ways ended up reinventing the wheel and not benefiting from the lessons of earlier generations of activists. There was also much less unity in views of what a new society free of injustice would look like.

The lack of intergenerational continuity aided the reemergence of third-path organizations during the 1960s. With the disintegration of the organized black left during the 1950s, influential author and activist Harold Cruse, like many others, began to construct a view of black liberation based on "black autonomy" (Gosse 2012).[11] These efforts would eventually result in the proliferation of third-path organizations during the 1960s. Small groups of black radical activists continued to try to find a future for black radicalism during the early 1960s in cities such as Detroit and New York (Gosse 2012). Organizationally weak, nevertheless they debated key issues, such as the role of whites in organizations committed to black liberation, that would roil the entire black power movement in the years to come. No consensus had emerged about the way forward for black radicalism, and the old black left remained relatively unorganized and very isolated from the mainstream of the growing black insurgency. A new generation of black activists without the organizational experiences of the previous generation would lead the new upsurge in the black liberation movement.

The sundering guaranteed that the next surge of black radicalism would look very different from the one in the first half of the twentieth century. Among organizational forms that were no longer active possibilities in the later period were black united fronts that included black liberals and leftists; black radical participation in a (mostly) unified labor movement; active labor support for racial equality (with the partial exception of the early civil rights movement, although even then labor played a large role in trying to *contain* black agitation); and efforts to build at least a semiunified progressive movement. At the same time, the later era had a stronger set of independent black political organizations with ties to the black grass roots, which not only helped drive both the civil rights and black power movements, with partially transformative results, but also provided significant support for activists when the state turned its full fury on black radicalism.

Lessons for Today?

American politics today has moved massively to the right as a result of the sundering. This situation is due in no small part to the isolation of African Americans from mainstream discourses on domestic politics and public policy. African Americans throughout the second half of the twentieth century were the strongest supporters of a social democratic agenda—an agenda that consistently attacked multiple forms of inequality and injustice—and when they were an active part of American political discourse, they helped move that discourse leftward. Another factor is that, from Frederick Douglass in the mid-nineteenth century through Du Bois and King in the twentieth, the black counterpublic was often the site of the most trenchant critiques of a very flawed American democracy. These trends continued as African Americans in the early twenty-first century supported the redistributive, progressive economic policies that radical liberals and leftists all supported before the sundering. Similarly, from Vietnam through Iraq, African Americans have proved to be the group of Americans most opposed to U.S. military intervention.[12] The defeat of black radicals during the 1970s aided the acceleration of the rightward shift, which was consolidated with the election of Ronald Reagan. With black speakers and black political speech demonized, a progressive force was removed from American political discourse.[13]

There are some lessons that we can apply to contemporary politics. One is that even devastating political eras are not permanent. In the midst of the latest right-wing wave, which has led to an even more degenerate state of global neoliberal politics and capitalist exploitation, this lesson is faintly heartening. As I argue elsewhere, there are substantial lessons, positive and negative, from the earlier periods of radical black insurgency that can be of help to political analysis and movements that remain committed to fighting against racial inequality and other forms of injustice (Dawson 2001, 2011).

A key lesson is that the political choices black radicals made were consequential, substantially contributing to the sundering and more generally to the decline of black radical movements in both periods of insurgency. McCarthyism, of course, devastated all sectors of the left, including the black left. Yet I agree with Arnesen (2012) when he assigns significant responsibility to the left itself. He is also correct when he suggests that the political program of the CPUSA during this period was in no small part responsible for the decline of the left and what I have called the sundering. Where he is very wrong is in his analysis of black politics and more generally the politics of race within the Leninist/CPUSA-dominated left. While he has a point when he argues that the language that the black left and its allies used to criticize black liberals during this period was harsh and quite probably often ill-considered, the substance of black liberals' claims about having been betrayed between 1947 and 1955 has been well documented by historians. While it is true that the black left often overlooked, ignored, or discounted the crimes of the Stalinist-era Soviet Union and the spread in central and eastern Europe after the war of what some labeled Soviet social imperialism, it is also the case that these same leftists' critique of the crimes of U.S. imperialism would prove to be on the mark, as demonstrated during the 1950s in Africa, Asia, and Latin America, where the United States was implicated in the overthrow of democratically elected governments, assassinations, and the backing of a set of puppet governments. Strangely, Arnesen emphasizes campaigns against white chauvinism as being the cause of the weakening of multiracial alliance without mentioning the attack that the CPUSA launched on work in support of black liberation. Instead of grappling with the changes in an economy that was increasingly pitting black workers against white workers at a time when blacks were seeking to make up ground after being excluded by both unions and management, Arnesen attacks policies designed to rectify the past and current injustices faced by midcentury black workers. These were difficult problems that faced progressive workers and their organizations, but to decline to address them in the name of a mythical working-class unity is to replicate in the twenty-first century the mistake of the American left that led to working-class division throughout the late nineteenth and twentieth centuries. Arnesen's racial dogmatism is displayed when he argues that the CPUSA's "civil rights initiatives—and Party policies–drove out white members" of the United Packinghouse

Workers locals in Chicago and Texas even though on the same page he cites in a footnote a passage claiming instead that what led to segregated facilities was "alarming signs of racial prejudice and segregation" among white workers, not the left's policies (Arnesen 2012, 38). Some lessons about how to build multiracial unity, it appears, have yet to be learned. To conclude, Arnesen is right when he states that the sundering did not end either the civil rights movement or black radical struggle more generally, but he severely underestimates how the character of those struggles was changed by the sundering. Radical possibilities that existed before the sundering no longer were perceived as being available a decade later—a perception that was dangerous inasmuch as it led to a narrowing of the radical imagination in black movements and many others. This is a problem that has only grown more severe over the past several decades.

More abstractly, the same point can be made in arguing against David Scott's rejection of "utopian" projects of "political and social change." He argues that since "we are [at] the virtual closure of the nationalist Bandung project that grew out of the anticolonial revolution, this story is an enfeebled and exhausted one" (Scott 2004, 30). I disagree that concepts such as self-determination must be discarded. Self-determination need not be bound to nationalist fantasies in the United States or elsewhere. It has been a central tenet of black political traditions that as long as white supremacy reigns and blacks are systematically disadvantaged, blacks have the right to determine their relationship to the polity and to society. As black leftists argued in the twentieth century, support for self-determination does not automatically entail support for racial separation or nationalism. Gary Wilder points to Aimé Césaire's controversial attempts to develop a program of anticolonialism in Martinique that did not have national independence as its goal. Right or wrong, Césaire's formulation called for a revolutionary transformation of the French Republic in order for it to be able to incorporate former colonies into the republic as fully equal partners. Wilder argues that Césaire attempted to universalize "republican universality by deracializing it" (Wilder 2009, 135), but Frederick Cooper demonstrates that key West African activists in the French colonies, such as Léopold Senghor, were also interpreting self-determination in a manner that was not at all tied to nation-state sovereignty (Cooper 2012).

The point to be made is that just as the periods of insurgency and mobilization may harbor unanticipated possibilities, what Wilder calls "futures that were once imagined but never came to be" may have "not yet realized emancipatory possibilities" that may "be recognized and reawakened as durable and vital legacies" in times of despair (Wilder 2009, 103). That is, by acting as if the impossible is possible, we may perhaps hasten its arrival. Contrast this view with the pessimism of David Scott, who argues that "after Bandung, after the end of anticolonialism's promise . . . we live in tragic times. . . . [The] critical languages in which we wagered our moral vision and our political hope (including, importantly, the languages of black emancipation and postcolonial critique) are no longer commensurate with the world they were meant to understand, engage, and overcome" (Scott 2004, 210). Using Scott's language, the period of the sundering was a "tragic" time—one that heralded the end of old alliances, old progressive politics. Yet a new era of black radicalism was only a decade off. This insurgency would take different forms than it did in the previous period, but it was transformative in its own right. There is no reason to think that we will never see another period of black radical insurgency. There is every reason to think that it will take very different forms, tackle different questions, and develop in directions as yet unforeseen. Given the ravages that white supremacy still produces (such as in the case of Trayvon Martin, an unarmed teenager who in February 2012 was shot by a neighborhood watch coordinator in a gated community in Sanford, Florida), we cannot afford to succumb to Scott's despair.

Wilder argues that for the activists of Césaire's time (1945–1962), the actors of the 1790s (the period of the Haitian revolution) and 1840s (the abolition of slavery in Martinique) were present and alive. My argument is that the sundering to a significant degree constituted a self-conscious attempt by the state and reactionary forces to erase Reconstruction, the pre–World War I period, and the 1930s from black politics and that this erasure was aided by many civil rights and labor leaders. They failed. Their successors also failed to fully erase the legacies of the black insurgencies of the 1960s and 1970s, despite the historical revisionism toward those times exemplified by the whitewashing of the legacies of Martin Luther King Jr. and Malcolm X. Those times are a part of our present, but so is the sundering. Thus, we have to understand and build new political movements that incorporate the lessons of the sundering as well as those of the insurgent traditions of the past. During the civil rights movement and black power eras, new paths were forged that laid the basis for contemporary black politics.

Black Power!

Our faded collective memories of the black-power-era mass insurgency are usually centered on the explosions in Watts (1965), in Detroit (1967), and then in more than a hundred American cities following the assassination of Martin Luther King Jr. on April 4, 1968. Yet the most salient and powerful feature of the black power era was not the spontaneous urban violence that occurred in the large cities of the North and West. The transformative component of the black power era was the incredibly deep and broad organizing of African Americans in all spheres of life. Militant blacks organized to gain power and effect change in military units stateside and in Vietnam, in hospitals, and on virtually every college campus from junior colleges such as Laney College in Oakland, California, to Ivy League institutions such as Harvard, Yale, and Cornell. Black communities themselves were organized on a massive scale. Not only were local black communities extremely well organized, but there was often regional coordination of activities, whether through regional student organizations, via metropolitan-area-wide alliances of militant black workers, or through the efforts of numerous nationalist and putatively Marxist organizations. Through some of these same mechanisms, but also through national networks, conferences, and newspapers with a national reach such as the *Black Panther* and *Muhammad Speaks,* the black power movement was also a nationwide phenomenon, with activists on one coast being aware of what was going on across the country. Only the civil rights movement had a more transformative effect on American institutions than the black power insurgency—and, like the civil rights movement, the black power insurgency sparked and inspired other movements within the borders of the United States.

I argued that a critical difference between the leftist politics of the early twentieth century and the black power era was that the latter period was marked by the proliferation of predominantly nonwhite radical organizations, most often Marxist, black nationalist, or some combination of the two. Not only was the CPUSA unable to provide leadership to this movement, but it actively criticized large segments of the movement as reactionary. Most especially, the backward position the CPUSA took toward the civil rights movement prevented the party from having even a small chance of regaining the influence in black communities that it squandered from the 1940s on. Further, by the time the black power movement was rising in influence, the Communist Party chose to meet the challenge of rising nationalist leaders such as Malcolm X by attacking *all* forms of nationalism as reactionary. In the 1970s—a time in which, one might have thought, the potential of some nationalist strands as engines of radical change would have been evident—Communist Party leader James Jackson wrote, "The main function of nationalism whatever its form is to split and divide and fragment the international working class and the advanced contingents of the national liberation movements" (Haywood 1978, 639).

These sentiments were evident to the black, Latino, and Asian American activists fighting in the streets during the 1960s and the first half of the 1970s. Yet these activists argued against the view that nationalism is always reactionary. First, black activists—even, perhaps particularly, black socialists—pointedly argued that organizing along racial lines was fueled not by nationalist dreams nor by middle-class desires to capture black markets but by the deep chauvinism (to use the polite term) of white workers who insisted on maintaining white privilege. Chicano and Puerto Rican activists often asserted that their movements were part and parcel of the worldwide anticolonial movement and explicitly aimed at the liberation of, respectively, Aztlán and Puerto Rico. Some Hawaiian activists made similar claims. While many Asian American activists did not explicitly make anticolonial claims for their movement, they too railed against the racial discrimination and chauvinism they encountered within the broader radical movement and also often had analyses similar to those of black and Latino activists. The key point is that large numbers of nonwhite radicals who considered themselves at least socialists and often Leninists argued that their movements were objectively revolutionary in their own right, since they were solidly aimed at the foundations of U.S. imperialism, and that organizational unity, particularly with white activists, must wait until their own movements and organizations were powerful enough to be able to minimize and overcome white chauvinism. Thus, they argued, their movements did not undermine working-class unity but indeed were the foundation for eventually building a stronger and truer unity. This point of view stands in stark contrast to the views of the CPUSA at the time, as advanced by theoreticians such as Jackson. Unlike Jackson and his comrades, this new generation of activists held that nationalism was not always reactionary. Indeed, nationalist movements could be in the vanguard of revolutionary movements.

Another major difference between the two periods of radical black insurgency, I argue, is that in the earlier period the Soviet Union had not yet been disgraced in the eyes of many leftists, and it provided the sole model for leftist movements to look to in the United States and elsewhere. By the 1960s, not only had Stalinism and the general disavowal of any focused work on people of color already led to the near collapse of the CPUSA in black communities, but with the rise of national liberation movements, particularly in Africa, and the non-European Marxist examples of Cuba, Vietnam, and preeminently China, there were other sources of inspiration and support to which one could turn. This different international context had a profound impact on the language of revolution that black militants adopted across radical ideologies. In this period of insurgency the language of national liberation and anticolonialism was used by a very wide range of groups and leaders. Instead of a focus on developing their own nation, black activists were more likely to use language referring to "internal colonialism." The change in language had important pragmatic and political implications. An emphasis on "national liberation" deemphasized language that would call for a broad multiracial class base alliance, for example. When alliances were formed, it was often between organizations and movements based in separate communities of color, each with its own narrative of colonialism and revolution.

The vacuum provided by the CPUSA was filled, mostly productively, by organizations dominated by nonwhite activists that were local, regional, and occasionally national in scope. These organizations developed out of the sweeping successes and bitter frustrations of the civil rights movement. The civil rights movement was a broader-ranging and more militant, albeit nonviolent, movement than generally acknowledged in today's popular discourse. The aims of the movement combined demands for the basic democratic, human, and citizenship rights that were suppressed by Jim Crow with a less well-known bundle of democratic demands tied to gaining economic justice for African Americans within the context of a racialized economy. As King explicitly argued, satisfying the latter set of demands would require state-mandated economic redistribution. Enormous victories were won due to the sacrifices of thousands of Americans, mostly but not exclusively African American. I have little patience for those—some on the left, some on the right—who claim that the civil rights movement was largely a failure. The dismantling of Jim Crow was one of the most deci- sive victories for democracy in American history, and it enabled and gave inspiration to a myriad of other democratic movements and initiatives within the United States.

Of course, the civil rights movement was also associated with tragedy, defeats, and frustrations. The escalating violence in the Deep South in 1963 and 1964 was one source of growing anger and concern for black activists organizing around voting and other civil rights in states such as Alabama and Mississippi. The refusal to seat the integrated Mississippi Freedom Democratic Party (MFDP) at the 1964 Democratic National Convention in favor of the segre- gated (and by party rules illegal) official delegation and to reduce MFDP participation to two nonvoting seats angered many of the younger activists working in the region. These activists viewed the negotiated compromise as a betrayal by the liberal establish- ment, including the civil rights leadership. John Lewis, at the time a leader of SNCC and later a member of Congress, argued in his autobiography:

> As far as I'm concerned, this was the turning point of the civil
> rights movement. I'm absolutely convinced of that. Until then,
> despite every setback and disappointment and obstacle we had
> faced over the years, the belief still prevailed that the system
> would work, the system would listen, the system would re-
> spond. Now, for the first time, we had made our way to the
> very center of the system. We had played by the rules, done
> everything we were supposed to do, had played the game ex-
> actly as required, had arrived at the doorstep and found the
> door slammed in our face. (Lewis and D'Orso 1998, 291)

The civil rights movement was a revolutionary social democratic phenomenon. The radical black social democratic movement that emerged out of the urban and rural South in the 1940s and 1950s, however, was largely based on sacred doctrine and organizations. As the violence mounted in the South, economic demands were ignored or rejected out of hand, and the civil rights movement was rebuffed by the nation's liberal white leaders, movement leaders found it increasingly difficult to address the growing anger within their own ranks as well as within smoldering large urban ghettos. As black southern activists, especially those in SNCC but also in organizations such as CORE, started discussing black power and transforming their organizations into exclusively black ones, the urban ghettos of the West and North were on the verge of rebellion. While the seeds of the black power era had been germinating for several years, one could argue with Lewis that the black power insurgency—particularly its organized component—was born on the floor of the Democratic National Convention in 1964.

These sentiments of rebellion were captured most eloquently by the black nationalist Malcolm X. Malcolm X was the most influential black leader of his time other than King. Particularly after his break with the Nation of Islam, Malcolm X advocated a brand of black nationalism that Hubert Harrison would have found deeply familiar. He demanded that blacks independently organize for black liberation, including fighting for the political, economic, and cultural control over their communities. Community control as well as other aspects of black liberation would entail having black power. He linked the black struggle for power to what he called the worldwide struggle for human rights, and he associated black liberation within the United States to the anticolonial struggles being waged around the world. Malcolm X also demanded that African Americans have the right to choose their political relationship to the United States—the right to self-determination.

The call for self-determination was central throughout the nineteenth and twentieth centuries. Both black nationalists such as Marcus Garvey as well as third-path organizations generations later, such as the Black Panther Party, saw the right to self-determination as the key political demand within their respective programs. Self-determination, however, was interpreted differently among black radicals. Many black nationalists linked the call for self-determination to a demand for the formation of a black state. This strand can be found in both conservative and revolutionary black nationalist demands from organizations such as the Nation of Islam and the Republic of New Africa. Black Marxists who advocated for self-determination were usually very careful to delink the demand for a state from the demand for self-determination. Black Marxists held that African Americans had the right to choose their relationship to the United States, but as Marxists, they often would argue against the formation of a black state even if they believed (as the CPUSA did in the 1930s) that blacks constituted a nation. National oppression (or, in more nationalist terms, racial oppression) was the context within which the demand for self-determination was justified. Also framed in this context were decisions from 1965 on by organizations central to the black freedom movement to restrict their leadership, and sometimes their membership, to members of black communities.

Malcolm X toward the end of his life, like Harrison, also started to identify capitalism as one of the sources of oppression worldwide in addition to racial oppression. Also like Harrison, he was unable to translate his vision for black politics into a stable organizational presence. In this case, his February 1965 assassination occurred before he could fully institutionalize his program. Malcolm X's fledging organization, the Organization for Afro-American Unity, never became solidly established or influential.

In the ensuing years black radicals from a wide range of traditions all claimed to be followers of Malcolm X. Even the right-wing Supreme Court justice Clarence Thomas claimed to be an admirer. The wide range of organizations and people claiming allegiance to the beliefs of Malcolm X is rooted in more than just naked opportunism (although that played a role then, as it does now). A very strong cultural conservatism that contained significant patriarchal elements was a consistent element of his thought, although toward the end of his life his thought began evolving rapidly, and he emphasized the need for a broad secular black movement even as he remained a devout Muslim. After his break with the Nation of Islam he embraced revolutionary nationalist positions; explicitly linked the black struggle for freedom to movements in Africa, Vietnam, and elsewhere in what then was known as the third world; and increasingly started to present analyses of capitalism as an oppressive economic system. The result was that many Marxists, particularly but not exclusively black Marxists, claimed Malcolm X as one of their own. His consistent emphasis on the need for blacks in the United States to know their own history, embrace their culture and reject that of the "oppressor," and develop ties to Africans and their struggles resonated with many cultural nationalists and pan-Africanists. Although he did not seem to see much of a contradiction between these various elements of his thought and program, they would evolve into distinct and often mutually hostile organized tendencies within the black liberation movement.

Out of the rage and sense of betrayal that Malcolm X articulated so well, several strands of black radical organizations developed. SNCC, which had been a central organization within the civil rights movement, would see development in both nationalist and leftist directions. Much of its better-known leadership would become associated with revolutionary nationalist organizations that combined black nationalism with variants of what was termed at the time "scientific socialism" or "African socialism."[14] Northern ghettos also saw the emergence of influential black nationalist organizations such as the Republic of New Africa and the East Coast–based Congress of African People. These organizations emphasized ties to Africa, generally saw whites as racist reactionaries, and advocated to various degrees economic and cultural independence and in some cases political separatism. The question of political independence and the formation of a black state, however, was as hotly contested among black nationalists as it was among black leftists.

Two of the most influential third-path organizations of the black power era were the Black Panther Party and the Detroit-based League of Revolutionary Black Workers. The Black Panther Party received far more media attention and attention from white radicals than any of the other groups. I will examine the Panthers' political platform in the next chapter, but briefly, they were self-described revolutionary nationalists and followers of Malcolm X. One of the more visible and controversial aspects of the Panthers' organizing was their emphasis on organizing street youth, and particularly the lumpen proletariat; another was their emphasis on armed self-defense.[15] Less noticed than their too often deadly confrontations with the police was a full range of social programs, including breakfast programs for children, health clinics, food programs, and the like. Much of the Panthers' work was predicated on building a strong community base and a political education program that went from street level on up. Arguably the most potent weapon in the Panthers' arsenal was their newspaper, the *Black Panther.* Truly nationwide in scope, it could be found in nearly every black community and was a source of information about the black movement in the United States as well as revolutionary movements around the world. It also served as a key propaganda organ, as important party policies were announced within the paper. Only *Muhammad Speaks,* the newspaper of the Nation of Islam, had as much or more influence than the Panthers' paper.

Eventually, increasingly violent confrontations with the state would combine with a deadly internal split to lead to the demise of the organization as a national force by 1972. The split within the Panthers was primarily between a faction that wanted to emphasize community service programs such as the free breakfast and medical clinic endeavors and a faction that wanted to emphasize the military aspects of revolution, take the party underground, and transform the organization into the Black Liberation Army. The split was deadly, with members of the two factions killing each other and in a few cases causing civilian casualties. The reasons for this enmity between factions included deep rivalries and suspicions between members of the top leadership as well as sustained counterintelligence work by U.S. intelligence agencies that was at least partly successful in raising the level of paranoia and provoking intraparty attacks. While the combination of violent state repression and severe internal dissension was unusually violent in the case of the Panthers, it would prove to be a deadly combination for black radical groups across the ideological spectrum.

Detroit's black leftists followed a different path and concentrated initially on organizing around the conditions black workers faced within the plants, particularly within the auto plants. Starting in one Dodge plant, the Dodge Revolutionary Union Movement eventually spread to plants throughout the local auto industry and eventually into workplaces of all types. The resulting League of Revolutionary Black Workers was eventually able to establish a strong base in a variety of workplaces, in the black community, and on college and high school campuses. They ended up confronting local government, management, and the UAW itself, and their influence extended beyond Detroit as radical black workers caucuses were formed from New Jersey to the Bay Area of California. The league's national influence was also enhanced through the writings of black Marxist theoretician James Boggs, an important early mentor for the group, as well as their own propaganda efforts.[16]

The league's film *Finally Got the News,* while widely shown, became a symbol of the internal strife that would tear apart the league all too quickly. There was considerable disagreement among the leadership about what path to take forward. The faction that wanted to build not only in the plants but in schools and black communities nationwide also wanted to forge strong alliances with white radicals and other radical forces; this group was widely seen as being associated with the film. The most diametrically opposed faction wanted to concentrate on organizing within the plants and focus on the issues directly facing the shop floor; initially this faction was also more nationalist in orientation. There were also important intermediate positions, as even those who saw the advantages of building alliances and organizing outside the plants cautioned that the perceived chaos associated with the rapid nationwide expansion of the Black Panthers suggested that it was a better idea to concentrate on local efforts until the organization was stronger and better prepared to maintain its cohesiveness and security while expanding. (Not the least important consequence of too rapid expansion, according to this faction, was the rapid loss of ideological cohesion and an increased vulnerability to state infiltration.) Another point of dispute was how to characterize white workers. Were they backward but part of the people, an element that could be won over, or were they hopelessly reactionary and should not be a focus of black leftists' work? The league's organizational split, which occurred in 1971 at about the same time as the Panther split but was considerably less violent, forestalled the possibility of forming a nationwide black Marxist organization, which many inside and outside the league saw as the next step in organizational development.

The splits within the Black Panther Party and the League of Revolutionary Black Workers were a devastating blow to the black liberation movement. The damage to these organizations signaled the demise of third-path groups capable of having a national reach and forging multiracial alliances while still maintaining their own independence. The Black Panther Party, particularly on the coasts, demonstrated a willingness and ability to reach out to and work with white, Puerto Rican, and Asian American radicals and revolutionaries. Detroit's population at the time was less racially diverse than the population in the Panthers' coastal strongholds, but Detroit black leftists also had a strong history of being able to work with white radical forces in and outside the plants. Whether organizations such as the Panthers or the

League of Revolutionary Black Workers would have been able to go beyond crafting alliances and participate in the building of multiracial radical organizations (as both groups claimed they wished to do at some point in their future) is unknown. What we do know is that a different organizational strategy would emerge by the middle 1970s—one that was more akin to that of the first period of black radical insurgency than the organizational path that had been largely followed during the first decade of the black power era.

There were dozens of other active black radical organizations ranging in size from small local collectives to organizations that had a significant local and in some cases regional and national presence, such as the Congress of African People (CAP). As the 1970s progressed, radicals from the black, Latino, and Asian American movements who remained active eventually converged on a more doctrinaire understanding of the working class and the relative place of struggles around racial justice (although they never completely abandoned or subordinated the latter work, as had happened in earlier generations). CAP provides an excellent example of the organizational trajectory followed by many black organizations, both small and large. Initially a cultural nationalist organization, over the years CAP moved into the ranks of those espousing scientific socialism, and eventually it would fully embrace Leninism and merge with other organizations that had roots in communities of color (primarily Asian American and Chicano), becoming the League of Revolutionary Struggle, which was part of the New Communist movement. Other black radical organizations would follow a similar path, affiliating with different communist organizations such as the Communist Workers Party or the Communist League.

Despite their differences, these organizations often engaged in a broad range of similar activities. They participated in the black arts movement, working with poets, musicians, playwrights, and other artists. All published newspapers that were widely read in their local communities as well as other publications (usually pamphlets). Service programs such as drug rehab, breakfast, education, and medical care were provided. The groups operated bookstores, founded study circles in every conceivable venue, made movies documenting their work, and engaged in support activities for many national liberation struggles not only in southern Africa but throughout the Third World. These organizations were deeply embedded on active-duty military bases, in a variety of workplaces, among black college students, and in nearly all black communities. One consequence of this shift was that organizations with large numbers of black radicals began to pull their cadres out of mass organizing in favor of internal organization building, a choice that dealt a major blow to black radicalism.

The last powerful effort of midcentury black radicalism was the African Liberation Support Committee (ALSC). The ALSC represented the final effective national alliance of black leftists and nationalists. Founded in 1972, the ALSC was a broad coalition of organizations and individuals originally formed to organize rallies in support of the liberation struggles of southern Africa. Throughout most of the 1970s these activities were supplemented in many areas by organizing around issues facing the local black community. In some locales one organization within the ALSC dominated; in others the local work was a result of coalition of organizations from a variety of ideological tendencies. The ALSC would decline for a variety of reasons, including the organizational disintegration that was affecting the black movement as a whole at the time and the withdrawal of black activists from mass organizing in favor of theory building and internal organizational work. Although important theoretical exchanges were held at the ALSC's national meetings and local work was often effective, the group left very little in the way of a lasting legacy. The Black United Front (BUF) of the late 1970s was an attempt to replicate ALSC's success along more general lines, but it was largely a top-down affair that involved debates among nationally and regionally prominent activists but was not based on robust local organizing and did not politically mobilize black communities. By this point the insurgency had been quiescent for years. The lack of ties to an active black movement and vibrant local organizations led the BUF to be predictably ineffective.

The 1970s also saw the emergence of a new organizational force in black radicalism. Black feminism had been an ideological tendency among African Americans going back to at least the nineteenth century. During the first half of the twentieth century, women such as Amy Jacques Garvey of the UNIA and Claudia Jones of the CPUSA fought for a black feminist perspective within these organizations. Women activists in the 1960s agitated for a black feminist perspective in organizations such as SNCC, the Black Panthers, and black student unions. By the early 1970s many black women were responding to what they viewed as the racism (and classism) within the women's movement and the sexism with the black movement by forming their own organizations and beginning to formalize theoretical and programmatic positions. Particularly true of early black feminist theorizing was an insistence on addressing at least minimally the intersection of race and gender, but for many feminist activists class and sexuality were important as well.[17] Organizing emerged at local levels around issues such as women's health, gender discrimination, incarceration, violence against women, and community issues such as environmental justice. The black feminist movement severely challenged conceptions of the "universal," whether it involved race, class, or gender. More analytically, black feminists, as did feminists more generally, challenged the notion that either the "color line" or capitalism represented an overarching system for organizing the world, instead arguing that the system of patriarchy predated the others. Marxists, including those who had emerged from the third-path organizations of the black power era, as well as most black nationalists rejected the view that patriarchy was an independent system of oppression that was just as systematic and important as the oppression generated by capitalism or a worldwide system of racial oppression. While black feminism would persist into the coming decades, it would also continue to face hostility from other ideological forces within the black community.

Black nationalism dissolved into several different tendencies. Those who did not convert to Marxism or remain revolutionary nationalists but did remain politically engaged often evolved into the active partners of ruling elites. Even organizations that embraced a relatively militant version of black power, such as the late 1960s version of CORE, often transformed into organizations espousing a conservative program and ideology. If not yet espousing a neoliberal program, their conservative organizational aspirations often led to an eventual degradation of a black power agenda. This version of "black power," which was often explicitly linked to black capitalism, still had too robust and militant a conception of politics to comfortably coexist with neoliberalism (Ferguson 2007). On the other hand, many adherents of nationalist versions of black power would end up working well within the policy and ideological framework developed by the same social engineers (some of whom were now prominent within the foundation world) who had conceived their modernization strategies within the context of the war in Indochina and were now applying them to the United States. Another tactical failure found among nationalist organizations (and the black left as well) was the constant removal of strong local leaders to national offices (for one example from CORE, see Ferguson 2007, 80). While many nationalist organizations remained influential among grassroots blacks far longer than the black left did, as a result of these and other problems they too would eventually end up marginalized.[18]

By the 1980s African Americans found themselves increasingly isolated politically. Within the polity they remained the most radical population along several dimensions, as the white population particularly, fueled in part by racial resentment, moved to the right and embraced the visions of Ronald Reagan and his successors. The Democratic Party from Jimmy Carter on would move to the right as well in an effort to capture a largely suburban white moderate vote. Growing tensions between communities of color were another factor that further isolated black politics. And without an organized radical wing (whether liberal, leftist, feminist, or nationalist) able to sustain political mobilization above the local level, African Americans found it increasingly difficult to influence political debate or rally in support of their own issues. As I describe in detail elsewhere, this process reached its nadir in the aftermath of Hurricane Katrina (Dawson 2011). By the dawn of the twenty-first century, black radicalism had a public face in the form of a number of independent public intellectuals as well as an online presence, and the combination of local forces and national mobilization (often aided by online efforts) could mobilize the black community for short periods in support of various issues. But black radicalism for the first time in a century had no substantial, sustained influence on the ground within a black politics that itself was greatly weakened.

Conclusion: Differences and Continuities between the Two Periods

One of the similarities between the two periods of heightened black radicalism in the twentieth century was the existence of a strong black civil society and an associated black public sphere (or counterpublic) within which political debate flourished.[19] In both periods, not only did churches, bookstores, block clubs, and other organizations provide an institutional base for black civil society and publics, but the movement itself strengthened black civil society by generating additional organizations such as black union caucuses, student organizations, radical newspapers, and community organizations.

Black radicals and their movements directly and explicitly challenged white supremacy during both periods. White supremacy was viewed as a racial order, a structure of oppression that shaped the very core of American life (including the organization of capitalism itself). Thus a central tenet embraced by black radicals of both periods was that the struggle for black freedom was a revolutionary struggle in its own right. The black leftist wing of black radicalism thereby, as noted earlier, embraced Marxism as a tool of black liberation. That said, there was little consensus among the black radicals of either period about whether blacks constituted a nation, and if so, what characteristics that nation had. Nevertheless, a wide range of black radicals of both periods embraced blacks' right to choose their future political relationship to the United States—the right to self-determination. The demand for self-determination remained critically important during both periods' black insurgencies. Another commonality found during both periods was that many who were initially attracted to black nationalism found themselves on a path toward becoming black leftists. Frequently this transformation came about because of perceptions that blacks needed allies and that a nationalist revolution was unlikely to be successful within the United States. The close correlation between black racial subordination and the severe economic disadvantage that was the lot of the great majority of blacks during this time simply fueled black radicals' attraction to Marxist analysis. Finally, viewing the black freedom struggle as part of a worldwide struggle against colonialism and imperialism led to an aggressive black internationalism. In particular, blacks saw as their strong allies the "dark nations of the world" (as it was phrased during first period) or their comrades in the third world (as the second period had it). This internationalism was found in both nationalist and leftist circles and was embraced not only by radical organizations but also by prominent individuals such as W. E. B. Du Bois.

The support that the CPUSA garnered at its most effective point and in the later era the deep support often earned by organizations such as the Black Panthers, the League of Revolutionary Black Workers, and countless others point both to a commonality between the two periods and to an important lesson for black radicals. Local support was strongest when Communist Party members took up basic issues such as unemployment and housing, fought against racial discrimination even within their own ranks, and organized to protect blacks from white violence regardless of whether it issued from the state or from civil society. Similarly, the black-power-era groups received their greatest support from the community when they organized local workers against discrimination on the shop floor or against local crafts unions that barred black entry, when they fought against police brutality, and when they provided basic services such as education and medical care that neither the capitalist economy nor the state provided. That is, support during both periods was greatest when the organizations to which black radicals belonged were seen as fighting to improve the everyday lives of "the people." A consequence of this deeper support was that in cities such as New York during the 1930s or Detroit during the black power era, black radicals (in the latter period both nationalist and leftist) were able to successfully use electoral campaigns to increase their influence and build black political power. The use of the electoral system for mobilization and education would not have been possible if black radicals had not already sunk deep roots in those communities.

A negative similarity between the two periods was that the predominantly white organizations of the New Left were no more successful in recruiting and retaining black activists or effectively working in black communities than the Communist and Socialist Parties of the earlier era had been. This failure was at least partly the result of hostility from large segments of white workers toward the black movement for freedom throughout the twentieth century. If the latter period's predominantly white social democratic organizations did not share the racism found among socialists during the earlier part of the century, they often shared their predecessors' predilection for downplaying the black freedom struggle. A predictable result was that social democracy in the United States remained racially bifurcated, with a strong, predominantly black and black-led wing (the civil rights movement being the

most powerful but not the only example of a black social democratic movement) and a relatively weak, predominantly white social
democratic wing that did not enjoy mass support after the second
decade of the century. In both periods, black leftists with Leninist
or social democratic tendencies encountered problems and severe
disagreements over the status of white workers. As Darrity (1989)
argues, "the problem of the white proletariat," with its suspicion
of black causes and often its open commitment to maintaining
white supremacy, made multiracial organizing in unions and workplaces exceedingly difficult. Equally problematic was the gap
between doctrine and reality, as black workers often looked askance
when groups that black Marxists were affiliated with aggressively
pushed for unity with whites who were often, although certainly
not always, racist.

Black leftists, and American leftists more generally, insufficiently
understood and theorized the changing relationship between the
racial order and the structure of the American economy. The first
period of black radicalism largely overlapped with the first Great
Migration of blacks from the South to the North, as industry's
demand for black labor increased with the launch of World War I,
which increased demand and also cut off European immigration
to the United States. After the end of the war, white veterans
wanted to expel black workers from their newly gained northern
jobs, which led to increased competition between black and white
labor and the racialization of the labor force as a racial order was
imposed within northern industry. Various occupations become
associated not only with gender but with race as well.[20] There was
an even more dramatic transformation of the relationship between
race and the economy during the second period of black radical insurgency. The apparent rise in black economic fortunes, including

the growth and diversification of the black middle class, masked dire developments within the structure of the American economy— what Thomas Holt calls "the reversal of prosperity" of the American economy, which soon "resembled a zero-sum game" (Holt 2010, 357). Blacks were concentrated in the sectors of the economy most vulnerable to the economic transformations of globalization and the conservative and neoliberal backlash—respectively, manufacturing and the state (Dawson 1994, 2001, 2011; Marable 2007; Holt 2010). By 1995 over half of all black professionals worked for the government, and by 1987 nearly one in four were unionized—a greater percentage than among whites (Holt 2010). As jobs left the cities for either overseas or the suburbs, economic devastation consumed black communities' economies. Holt states, "By the early 1970s the central city's share of the total industrial jobs in the country's twelve largest metropolitan areas 'dropped from 66.1 percent in 1946 to less than 40 percent in 1970.' Residential apartheid and economic deprivation went hand in hand" (Holt 2010, 348). The declining American economy provided the conditions for increased white resistance to black economic advancement and made whites a promising target for right-wing political mobilization. Yet even though the black left had an undertheorized understanding of the dynamics of the American economy, it was generally far superior to that of the white left, since it at least incorporated some aspects of racial subordination into its analysis and consequently was better able to formulate strategies for multiracial and workplace organizing. In neither period, however, was there a sufficiently sophisticated analysis of how the changing American economy and its interaction with the racial order shaped the possibilities for black radical organizing.

The extraordinary changes in the American political economy and demographics due to the second Great Migration of blacks to the North and West changed blacks' relationship to the economy. Blacks became incorporated into the manufacturing and state sectors and became much more directly involved in labor organizing around both worker and racial issues. It was this transformation of the black workforce that led to the growth of shop floor organizing by a variety of black radical forces during the black power era. The racial structure of the economy, even if incompletely understood, led organizers to demand, for example, "super-seniority" within unions—a protective device for black workers who had been excluded from unions because of race and thus were vulnerable to being the first laid off (Sugrue 2008). One implication for today is that as manufacturing continues to move offshore and public workers have become subject to political attack, any modern black movement must reanalyze blacks' relationship to the current economy and readjust demands and strategies accordingly; the type of widespread labor organizing in the manufacturing sector that occurred among blacks in the 1960s and 1970s will no longer be possible.

Black radical movements in every period, not just the ones discussed here, suffered extremely high levels of violence from the state in the form of its police and counterintelligence agencies (such as the infamous COINTELPRO program of the FBI that targeted both the civil rights and black power movements for disruption, discrediting, and destruction) and from white civil society (sometimes in the form of explicitly racist organizations such as the Ku Klux Klan, often in the form of violence perpetrated by unorganized white citizens). The violence was particularly constant and terroristic in the South but was common throughout the United States. Throughout the century assassinations, bombings, ambushes, and a variety of other methods were used in an attempt to physically destroy organizing efforts by and on behalf of blacks and did not really decline until the movements themselves died out in the last quarter of the century (and even then they never completely vanished). Entire organizations such as the NAACP in the South and the Communist Party would either disappear or be driven underground for years at a time. Just as debilitating as the violent attacks on the movements, and coordinated with them, was the incessant subjection of black radicals to the judicial system— tying up resources and activists for years even when the activists escaped punitive prison sentences.

Another crippling continuity was the continued organizational weaknesses caused by sexist attitudes and practices that were prevalent among black male leadership (and activists more generally) institutionalized within organizations, and sometimes even formalized within political programs. The Panthers, with their masculinist approach to politics, were particularly known for their sexism, which sometimes reached vile and violent levels, as was also occasionally the case in SNCC. The problem, however, was found throughout the movement, and women leaders and activists left many movement organizations due to sexism. The organized black feminist response during the second period, however, represented a stark difference in how patriarchal practices were viewed in the two eras. The black feminist response emerged at a time when feminists throughout the world were challenging patriarchy as a fundamental system of oppression that intersected with other systems of subordination, such as those structured by class and race. The prominence of a strong racial order in the United

States alongside systems of class and gender subordination pro-vided the conditions that enabled the development of an American black feminist movement (as well as the parallel but not identical feminist movements of other women of color within the United States).

Arguably, the differences between the two periods of intense black radical activism were more significant than the similarities. First, during the black power era there was no dominant national leftist organization like the Socialist Party before World War I or the Communist Party after the early 1920s. One consequence of this fact, as has been shown, was that in the black power era there was an extremely wide range of active, influential, and effective radical organizations not only in black communities, in work-places, and on college campuses but also among other people of color. A further consequence was that it was a period of innovation and experimentation, of institution building, of giddy highs and hellish lows. After the transition from the civil rights movement to the black power era there was also no dominant ideological ten-dency. Black nationalists, black Marxists, radical liberals, and black feminists all battled on behalf of their viewpoints, ideologies, and programs. Unlike the previous period, these battles took place not just among the leadership but also in grassroots organizations, in communities, and (to invoke the title of Melissa Harris-Lacewell's 2004 book) in barbershops and churches, if not yet on BET.

While the presence of a robust black civil society was a similar-ity between eras, those civil societies— and the black movements that drew on them—displayed some notable differences. The losses due to McCarthyism in the decade following World War II and the purging of leftists from both labor and civil rights organizations meant that the civil rights and labor movements were far more separated from each other, as leftist activists had previously served as a link between them. Second, black united fronts in the earlier period typically included alliances between black liberals and black leftists, with nationalists being largely absent. During the black power era, by contrast, united fronts more often included alliances between nationalists and leftists, as in both the ALSC and the BUF. Yet a weakness found during both periods was a tendency for radical organizations, both nationalist and leftist, to build black united fronts from the top down. While this brought together key organizations and leaders from throughout the country, it also meant that these organizations had relatively shallow roots within black communities (Marable 2011).

Another critical difference was that in the latter period international leftism was far more severely split than it had been in the earlier era. Not only had the Soviet Union been discredited in the eyes of radical activists inside and outside the black movement, it had a serious and hostile rival in Maoist China. Radical organizations, black and others, chose sides, with morally reprehensible if predictable results (more on this in the next chapter). The black power movement was organized in the midst of the anticolonial and national liberation movements. The changed international context provided an entirely new language of revolution. Demands for liberation of blacks and for black political power by individuals such as Malcolm X and organizations such as the Black Panther Party had a very different valence than did cries for working-class unity and slogans such as "Unite and fight," which had been popularized by the CPUSA.

Relatedly, in the second period there was a more diffuse theoretical understanding of what constituted Marxism. The study of Marxist and non-Marxist theoreticians from the third world meant that there was not the same degree of shared theoretical heritage among black radicals that had existed previously. Plus the emphasis on Maoism had theoretical and practical consequences. The Maoist concept, found in key works such as Mao Zedong's *On Contradiction* and *On Practice,* that knowledge came from the people and even more so from practice (practical work) meant a shift in many black circles away from works such as Marx's *Capital* to Lenin's *What Is to Be Done* and of course Mao's oeuvre. While there were still some theoretical debates, such as over the status of blacks within the United States (usually under the rubric of the "national question"), there was much less theoretical focus in the second period than in the first.

A powerful set of differences flowed from the fact that the most influential black nationalist during the first era had been Marcus Garvey while Malcolm X had that role during the black power era (even though both leaders were personally out of the picture, due to imprisonment and exile in Garvey's case and assassination in Malcolm X's, by the time black leftist radicalism had reached its heights). Garvey attacked with great vigor and bile black leftists and liberals (as he himself was attacked). Thus hard lines were drawn between the nationalist and leftist camps. Malcolm X, on the other hand, reached out to a variety of radical forces and thus laid the ideological basis for some level of cooperation between radical forces. It is important to note that Garvey was largely procapitalist, while by the end of his life Malcolm X was clearly opposed to capitalism; this anticapitalism served as another potential area of agreement among diverse black radical forces in the second period. In addition, Malcolm X's ideology over the last year of his life shifted toward socialist ideas, if not socialism itself, making more respectable a path toward Marxism that many black nationalists would take a decade later. Thus the differences between the two leading nationalists of their times had a critical effect in shaping the possibilities for cooperation between radical black nationalists and leftists. During the first half of the twentieth century the CPUSA arguably enjoyed its strongest support in black communities such as Harlem and Chicago. Two generations later, progressive movements were launched by the social democratic civil rights movement, and the militant left was fueled and often led, including in its final New Communist phase, by organizations and individuals with roots in the radical movements that emerged from the burning ghettos and barrios of urban America. Yet the hostility that white workers during both periods often evinced toward organizing for black justice, as well as the nearly constant tendency for dominant sections of the white left to underplay and underestimate the vitality and centrality of black and parallel movements, meant that American progressive and radical movements throughout the century were seriously crippled and far weaker than they should have been, and much less powerful than their European analogues. During the second period labor hostility toward black radicalism was further institutionalized through the policing of the civil rights movement by the liberal labor movement. For example, in 1960 the fledging student leadership of SNCC withdrew an invitation to Bayard Rustin to speak at a conference due to pressure from the AFL-CIO leadership, which objected both to Rustin's left-wing politics as well as to his homosexuality (Marable 2011). The entire range of progressive movements, including the women's, socialist, and old and New Left movements, suffered as a result of these failings. Consequently, any history of radical America should have as one of its central themes the role of race in the rise and decline of progressive movements. As radical movements declined across the board during the 1970s and the country moved rapidly to the right, a discussion began in both academic and radical circles about why the various radical and progressive movements had been so decisively defeated. In the next chapter I turn the debate over who and what killed the left.

Chapter 3

Who and What Killed the Left

Who or what did kill the left? For a number of academics and former activists, it was the turn to identity politics. In particular, the black power movement was what led to the demise of a vibrant left in the last decades of the twentieth century.

For example, Brubaker and Cooper claimed:

> From the late 1960s on, with the rise of the Black Power movement, and subsequently other ethnic movements for which it served as a template, concerns with and assertions of identity, already linked . . . to "communal culture," were readily, if facilely, transposed to the group level. The proliferation of identitarian claim-making was facilitated by the comparative institutional weakness of leftist politics in the United States and by the concomitant weakness of class-based idioms of social and political analysis. . . . [T]he weakness of class politics in the United States . . . left the field particularly wide open for the profusion of identity claims. (Brubaker and Cooper 2000, 3)

This tied in with what Gitlin claimed was the reason the left dissolved:

> There was a sea change in political culture. If society as a whole seemed unbudgeable, perhaps it was time for special-ized subsocieties to rise and flourish. For this reason if no other, the universalist impulse was fractured again and again. In the late 1960s, the principle of separate organization on behalf of distinct interests raged through "the movement" with amazing speed. On the model of black demands came those of feminists, Chicanos, American Indians, gays, lesbi-ans. One grouping after another insisted on the recognition of difference and the protection of their separate and distinct spheres. . . . From the 1970s on, left-wing universalism was profoundly demoralized. (Gitlin 1995, 100–101)

According to this view, the demise in universalism came with an increasing fragmentation in the movement, a retreat to a politics of culture and identity, and a lack of concern about fundamental economic issues, all of which led to a deep resentment on the part of working-class white men (and, I would argue, middle-class ones too), who believed that their interests and oppression no longer mattered and were thus justifiably attracted to the right wing, which, first under the surprisingly successful segregationist Alabama governor and presidential candidate George Wallace and then under Richard Nixon, fanned racial resentment in the late 1960s.[1] This group constituted the core of what was then called Nixon's "silent majority" (as well as of his and the Repub-lican Party's southern strategy) and later evolved into the core of the Reagan Democrats. Thus, Gitlin concluded, the black power movement was ultimately responsible both for the fragmentation of the left, as all of these other movements copied it, and for the move to the right that foreclosed progressive change for at least a generation, directly leading to conservative triumph in America.

I disagree with this interpretation. I argue that such a perspective presents a blatantly false picture of the black movements of the 1960s and early 1970s. This perspective is false in the sense that factually the history is wrong, and it is also false in the sense that the content of black political thought and practice from that period does not fit the critics' description of it. Theoretically, these critics advance a false universality; one that, far from being transcendent, is actually based on the interests and standpoint of the historically privileged group. These are not just questions of striving for historical and theoretical fidelity, although this is an important concern; these are questions that shape the perceptions of current activists, organizations, and theorists striving to rebuild various progressive movements. These concerns are at the heart of our theoretical, practical, and normative understanding of the state and future of the left in the United States.

In my critique I will focus on Rorty's version of this argument, which he presented in his Massey Lectures of 1997 and which were published in 1998 as *Achieving Our Country: Leftist Thought in Twentieth Century America*. I focus on Rorty because his interpretation is one of the more sophisticated ones, is historical, and covers a wide range of themes. He also makes a bold claim that "the period between 1910 and 1964, [is] the period which I think of as American leftism at its best," even though he himself was anti-Soviet (Rorty 1998, 65). I also focus on Todd Gitlin's arguments, particularly as presented in his 1995 book *The Twilight of*

Common Dreams: Why America Is Wracked by Culture Wars. Gitlin is not only a prominent sociologist and chronicler of the New Left but also one of the central early leaders of the New Left, and so his interpretations have been influential across the political spectrum.

The Cultural Turn and the Specter of Identity Politics

The cultural left inherited the slogan "Power to the people" from the Sixties Left, whose members rarely asked about how the transference of power was supposed to work. This question still goes unanswered.
—RICHARD RORTY

Rorty demonstrated a lack of knowledge of a wide range of black-power-era groups, all of whose programs had clear ideas about the "transference of power." Had he been familiar with movements of the late 1960s, he would have known that there were a myriad of proposed scenarios for such a transference; from the perspective of today, some of them are fanciful and most are unacceptable, but all of them are fully in line with what a young radical movement would develop. Besides, some of the most radical black organizations, such as the Black Panther Party for Self-Defense, had fully developed reformist agendas, as we shall see. Furthermore, Rorty's consciousness might have ended in the 1960s, but black radicalism was still a potent force well into the 1970s and became a central component of the New Communist movement that persisted throughout the 1970s. Perhaps a question that Rorty should have answered (one that I began to address in the last chapter) was which "people" we are talking about.

We begin to see Rorty's answer in the following quote from his essay in defense of ethnocentrism, which makes clear that at least along some dimensions he has an extremely narrow definition of "the people"—a definition consistent with another argument found in his writings, where he makes it clear that political change comes from well-meaning elites, not from mass action. The people, at least those who count, are his peers and other members of the elite—to use his language, the members of "your club."

> You cannot have an old-timey *Gemeinschaft* unless everybody pretty well agrees on who counts as a decent human being and who does not. But you *can* have a civil society of the bourgeois democratic sort. All you need is the ability to try and control your feelings when people who strike you as irredeemably different show up at City Hall, or the green-grocer, or the bazaar. When this happens, you smile a lot, make the best deals you can, and, after a hard day's haggling, retreat to your club. There you will be comforted by your equals. (Rorty 1991, 253–253)

This is the point of view of one used to privilege and preserving that privilege—the privilege of not having to deal with those not one's "equals." This is an unacceptable view of a democratic polity, although today we are far from meeting even Rorty's exceedingly minimal standards. Given Rorty's stated preference for the quietude of a private club and elite-driven change, we should not be surprised that the movements of the late 1960s—the ones that were rude, loud, and unruly and demanded "power to the people"—did not find favor in his eyes. It is not surprising, therefore, that Rorty's preferred leftist era was by his own admission one of the whitest I will discuss.

Rorty did admit that the period between 1910 and 1964, which he saw as the height of radicalism in the United States, had some drawbacks—for example, there was dismissive treatment of women by the white male left, as well as what he describes as the "brutal[ity]" with which gays and lesbians were viewed. He also said there was a complete refusal by his reformist left for *four decades* to take on black oppression—in order, according to Rorty, to keep the southern wing of the Democratic Party within the progressive coalition. The reformist left was also "blissfully unaware that brown-skinned Americans in the Southwest were being lynched, segregated, and humiliated in the same way as were African-Americans in the Deep South" (Rorty 1998, 75). He then made the following incredible statement:

> From the point of view of today's Left, the pre-Sixties Left may seem as callous about the need of oppressed groups as was the nation as a whole. *But it was not really that bad.* For the reformist Left hoped that the mistreatment of the weak by the strong in general, and racial discrimination in particular, would prove to be a by-product of economic injustice. . . . They saw prejudice against those groups as incited by the rich in order to keep the poor from turning their wrath on their economic oppressors. The pre-Sixties Left assumed that as economic inequality and insecurity decreased, prejudice would gradually disappear. (Rorty 1998, 75–76; emphasis added)

And Rorty wondered why the leftists of the 1960s and 1970s thought that what he called the reformist left was bankrupt? More analytically, his understanding of the origins of, for example, black oppression during the century that followed the Civil War is historically shallow and clueless when it comes to understanding black political thought. There was far more to black oppression during that period than just the dividing of the working class. He did not understand the role played by the superexploitation of black workers (and black people more generally), not only on the plantations and in the factories of the Jim Crow South but in the Fordist-era factories of the North, Midwest, and West as well.

Rorty made a moral judgment when he argued that "it was not really that bad." Linda Zerilli asked a question that Rorty, with his lack of self-reflexivity, clearly did not consider: how should one judge?[2] She argued that,

> rather than search for a universal (shared) core, occupy the place of the other, or sanctify the idea that no outsider is in a position to understand or judge the other, outsideness suggests that we understand and judge from a position that is neither identical nor incommensurable but rather mediated, at once separate from and related to that which we judge. Outsideness works both ways: just as we raise questions for a foreign culture (or people) that it does not raise for itself, so that foreign culture (or people) raises questions for us—if we allow it to do so. Outsideness as a condition of judging, then, entails a willingness to allow the encounter with others to raise questions about our own norms and practices. (Zerilli 2009, 314)

Rorty did not judge his preferred reformist left from the perspective of those who continued to be brutalized during that period. He took his own point of view as normative and privileged—which has been the common practice of the reformist left from the early days of the Socialist Party. Jim Crow really was that bad, the bitter fruit that Billie Holiday sang about—the thousands of lynched African Americans–just one grim indicator of how bad it really was.

Rorty turned to Freud when admitting that the 1960s left might have been right about the deep psychological roots of what he calls "sadism" toward blacks. Unlike Du Bois, however, Rorty never was able to analytically combine the economic superexploitation of blacks and other subordinate groups within the United States with psychological phenomena as integral pieces of the racial order. Rorty and his ilk were seemingly incapable of seeing the question of economic exploitation and how it intersected with other aspects of exploitation except from the standpoint of white males. If he had been willing and able to analyze these phenomena from the location Zerilli advocated, he would have understood what James Boggs, the 1960s black autoworker and Marxist theoretician, conceptualized so well as early as 1963: "In most countries the struggle of the oppressed has a class character only. But in the United State the Negroes have not only been at the bottom of the economy, they have been kept there on a race basis. Therefore, it is not just the economic system against which the Negro struggles, as many Marxists would have it" (Boggs 1970, 28).

Further, if Rorty had paid attention to the non–white-male-dominated components of the left, he might have been surprised by one of the less doctrinaire but easily identifiable and extremely well-known manifestos of a segment of the New Left: the ten-point program of the Black Panther Party. This manifesto is not about ending sadism. It is about ending oppression, including economic exploitation—it was the social democratic program of a self-described revolutionary nationalist organization. It was a program consistent with the dual approach (attacking regimes of economic exploitation and racial subordination, although not usually patriarchy) that Boggs and so many other black-power-era theoreticians advocated. It was also a program typical of numerous third-path organizations, from the Liberty League and the African Blood Brotherhood in the early twentieth century through the Black Panther Party and the League of Revolutionary Black Workers in the black power era.

Todd Gitlin also lamented the transformations that ensued as the black movement transitioned to one dominated by various strains of black power. Gitlin, however, waxed nostalgic about a different era than Rorty did. He identified the period of the civil rights movement, combined with that of the early New Left, as the period during which progressives of all races and ethnicities strived to build a truly universal movement. According to Gitlin, the most important New Left organization, the predominantly white Students for a Democratic Society (SDS), revived the idea of an enlightenment-based idea of the universal. He argued that the black power movement destroyed the universalist impulse, particularly as a wide range of groups came to emulate its separatist philosophy and organizational strategies.

The seeds of this disastrous turn of events, however, could be found earlier in the civil rights movement despite its seemingly universalist demands emphasizing democratic inclusion. The civil rights movement, according to Gitlin, contained a dangerous impulse:

> To oppose racial oppression was to affirm that everyone had
> the right to sit at the same lunch counter, to vote at the same

voting booth, to sit in the same seats on the bus, and swim in the same pool. But civil rights actions embodied another objective as well: the experience of community and solidarity. Ostensibly a means to secure equal rights, solidarity also turned out to be an end in itself. In the experience of the mass meeting, the organization of the boycott of buses and stores, *fraternité* manifested itself alongside *liberté*. Civil Rights activists spoke unabashedly of the "beloved community," as did their student radical allies in the largely white New Left. (Gitlin 1995, 86–97)

What was the dangerous seed sown during the civil rights movement that undermined and eventually, with the advent of black power, destroyed universalist sentiments, to the ongoing detriment of those on the left? It was Martin Luther King Jr.'s concept of "beloved community," which blossomed into the black movement's embrace of black solidarity and the ensuing fragmentation of the left. Black solidarity led to particularism and eventually nationalism. This progression from "beloved community" to full-fledged black nationalism was inevitable because the concept of "beloved community" led to people taking joy from and wanting to work with people of their own kind.

Gitlin's understanding of the "beloved community" is very different from that of its originator. King explained the concept in a 1957 SCLC newsletter: "The ultimate aim of SCLC is to foster and create the beloved community in America where brotherhood is a reality. . . . [the] SCLC works for integration. Our ultimate goal is genuine intergroup and interpersonal living—integration" (King 1957). Years later King amplified the original concept: "Our loyalties must transcend our race, our tribe, our class, and our nation" (King 1986a, 253). This is not a statement about black solidarity, let alone black nationalism, and it is bizarre that Gitlin saw it as such. For both Gitlin and Rorty, the black insurgencies of the 1960s and 1970s led directly to the abandonment of the left's universalist aspirations and then its inevitable fragmentation.

The critics' retelling of that history does not conform with the history of the black power movement as documented by historians. For example, the person who could be considered the first national spokesman of the black power movement, Malcolm X, embedded a critique of capitalism within his teachings—a critique that continued to deepen in theory and practice with the emergence of organizations such as the Black Panther Party and the League of Revolutionary Black Workers, eventually becoming a central element of the black power movement. Political theorist Wendy Brown asked, "What does politicized identity want?" (Brown 1995, 62). A more useful framing, perhaps, is to ask what oppressed people want (to use Iris Young's language), or what dominated people want (to use Philip Pettit's). Put in these terms, the answer is not so different from that of oppressed or dominated working-class people: freedom, political power, an egalitarian redistribution of resources, and the other demands that a politicized working class has historically advanced. The observation that oppressed groups are not mutually exclusive sets (women, blacks, workers, etc.) only serves to reinforce this last point (Young 1990; Pettit 1997). As we will examine in more depth later in this chapter, the overlap between the core concerns of black-power-era demands for justice and those of classic socialism suggests that the ability to put forth demands for a universal transformation of the entire system is not necessarily the preserve of any one social group.

A revolutionary nationalist organization, the Black Panther Party, provides an example of how particularistic demands were capable of demanding a transformation so fundamental as to require the dismantling of multiple systems of subordination, not just racial subordination. The Panthers proposed an advanced social democratic program, and despite its significant shortcomings, it was as important as what any other organization—old left, New Left, black power, civil rights, or Rorty's own reformist left—was advocating at the time. These were the Black Panther Party's demands:

1. We Want Freedom. We Want Power to Determine the Destiny of Our Black Community.
    We believe that Black people will not be free until we are able to determine our destiny.

2. We Want Full Employment for Our People.
    We believe that the federal government is responsible and obligated to give every man employment or a guaranteed income. We believe that if the White American businessmen will not give full employment, then the means of production should be taken from the businessmen and placed in the community so that the people of the community can organize and employ all of its people and give a high standard of living.

3. We Want an End to the Robbery by the Capitalists of Our Black Community.
    We believe that this racist government has robbed us, and now we are demanding the overdue debt of forty acres and two mules. Forty acres and two mules were promised 100 years ago as restitution for slave labor and mass murder of Black people. We

*will accept the payment in currency which will be distributed to
our many communities. The Germans are now aiding the Jews
in Israel for the genocide of the Jewish people. The Germans
murdered six million Jews. The American racist has taken part in
the slaughter of over fifty million Black people; therefore, we feel
that this is a modest demand that we make.*

4. We Want Decent Housing Fit for the Shelter of Human
   Beings.
   *We believe that if the White Landlords will not give decent
   housing to our Black community, then the housing and the land
   should be made into cooperatives so that our community, with
   government aid, can build and make decent housing for its
   people.*

5. We Want Education for Our People That Exposes the True
   Nature of This Decadent American Society. We Want
   Education That Teaches Us Our True History and Our
   Role in the Present-Day Society.
   *We believe in an educational system that will give to our people a
   knowledge of self. If a man does not have knowledge of himself
   and his position in society and the world, then he has little chance
   to relate to anything else.*

6. We Want All Black Men to Be Exempt From Military
   Service.
   *We believe that Black people should not be forced to fight in the
   military service to defend a racist government that does not
   protect us. We will not fight and kill other people of color in the
   world who, like Black people, are being victimized by the White
   racist government of America. We will protect ourselves from the*

force and violence of the racist police and the racist military, by whatever means necessary.

7. We Want an Immediate End to Police Brutality and Murder of Black People.

   We believe we can end police brutality in our Black community by organizing Black self-defense groups that are dedicated to defending our Black community from racist police oppression and brutality. The Second Amendment to the Constitution of the United States gives a right to bear arms. We therefore believe that all Black people should arm themselves for self-defense.

8. We Want Freedom for All Black Men Held in Federal, State, County and City Prisons and Jails.

   We believe that all Black people should be released from the many jails and prisons because they have not received a fair and impartial trial.

9. We Want All Black People When Brought to Trial to Be Tried in Court by a Jury of Their Peer Group or People from Their Black Communities, as Defined by the Constitution of the United States.

   We believe that the courts should follow the United States Constitution so that Black people will receive fair trials. The Fourteenth Amendment of the U.S. Constitution gives a man a right to be tried by his peer group. A peer is a person from a similar economic, social, religious, geographical, environmental, historical and racial background. To do this the court will be forced to select a jury from the Black community from which the Black defendant came. We have been, and are being, tried by all-White juries that have no understanding of the "average reasoning man" of the Black community.

10. We Want Land, Bread, Housing, Education, Clothing, Justice and Peace.

When, in the course of human events, it becomes necessary for one people to dissolve the political bands which have connected them with another, and to assume, among the powers of the earth, the separate and equal station to which the laws of nature and nature's God entitle them, a decent respect of the opinions of mankind requires that they should declare the causes which impel them to the separation.

We hold these truths to be self-evident, that all men are created equal; that they are endowed by their Creator with certain inalienable rights; that among these are life, liberty, and the pursuit of happiness. That, to secure these rights, governments are instituted among men, deriving their just powers from the consent of the governed; that, whenever any form of government becomes destructive of these ends, it is the right of the people to alter or abolish it, and to institute a new government, laying its foundation on such principles, and organizing its powers in such form, as to them shall seem most likely to effect their safety and happiness. Prudence, indeed, will dictate that governments long established should not be changed for light and transient causes; and, accordingly, all experience hath shown that mankind are more disposed to suffer, while evils are sufferable, than to right themselves by abolishing the forms to which they are accustomed. But, when a long train of abuses and usurpations, pursuing invariably the same object, evinces a design to reduce them under absolute despotism, it is their right, it is their duty, to throw off such government, and to provide new guards for their future security. (Dawson 2001, 114)

Despite its significant omissions, most tellingly the absence of gender issues (not surprising given the organizational and personal histories of the leadership), this program could not be won without a revolution, even if a nonviolent one. It would have taken a revolutionary movement on the scope of the civil rights movement to achieve these goals. Yet while we can object to some of the demands, it is still the case that nearly all could be read as belonging to a social democratic agenda. The Panthers were very self-conscious on that point. In part, their aim, as they saw it, was to educate people about what it would take to make what most in the black community at the time viewed as reasonable changes to our society and polity. As my survey research in *Black Visions* demonstrated, as of the mid-1990s a large majority of African Americans still would have supported a clear majority of the planks in the Panther program. Further, this program had enormous influence beyond the black movement, including in Chicano, Puerto Rican, and Asian American radical organizations and collectives. It had substantial influence in the white segment of the New Left as well.

Organizations that emerged out of the breakup of SDS themselves split in some cases over support for the Panthers, and a number of white organizations emerged to support the Panthers. The Black Panther Party's program was social democratic but not particularly liberal. Not all of the program's demands can be accommodated relatively straightforwardly within a liberal framework; point number three, demanding reparations, would be particularly hard to achieve.

Nevertheless, three things can be said about the Panther agenda. One is that the Panthers were not concerned primarily with recognition and identity. The Panthers and their many, many supporters (in 1969 the Panthers were identified in a Harris Poll by black respondents as being likely the most important black organization of the future) wanted power, the radical redistribution of resources, and self-determination—an agenda that leftists across the decades and around the world, social democratic and Leninist, would recognize as being akin to their own agendas.

Which brings me directly to my second point: just as this agenda was not primarily about identity, culture, and recognition, neither was it centered on the fight against sadism, as Rorty argued. Finally, as I have already alluded to, it cannot be said that the Panthers and other similar black radical organizations, as well as more doctrinaire ones, were unfocused on key economic issues, including in many cases organizing at the point of production as well as being deeply involved in organizing workers. It should also be remembered that the Black Panthers, along with the League of Revolutionary Black Workers and other organizations, organized black workers in cities such as Chicago, Detroit, and Pittsburgh to protest not just racist practices by white workers but, more important, the white supremacist policies of northern trade unions.

A further problem in Rorty's analysis is characteristic of those who were severe critics of the black power movement and regarded black nationalism with abject horror. While describing the differences between James Baldwin and the Honorable Elijah Muhammad (of the Nation of Islam), both harsh critics of white people and of white supremacy within the United States, Rorty argued: "The difference between Elijah Muhammad's decision about how to think of America and the one reached by Baldwin is the difference between deciding to be a spectator and to leave the fate of the United States to the operation of nonhuman forces, and deciding to be an agent. . . . Neither forgave, but one turned away from the project of achieving the country and the other did not" (Rorty 1998, 13).

Rorty had part of the analysis right in the sense that the Nation of Islam, led first by Muhammad (who was assisted for a time by Malcolm X) and later by Louis Farrakhan, did reject the United States as it was constituted, considering it corrupt to its core. So too did many black nationalists and their organizations, black leftists and their organizations, and the activists of many other races and ethnicities, including important segments of the New Left. Rorty would not have disagreed with that statement.

What I object to is characterizing these groups and individuals en masse as having given up agency and become mere spectators. Many institutions that had to deal with activist groups between 1964 and 1980—including private sector organizations; state entities such as the police, military, or governments at all levels of the federal system; entities embedded within civil society such as the UAW or mainstream Christian churches; and hundreds of universities—would have bitterly testified that these activist groups had not given up their agency, and certainly they would have wished that these groups had been mere spectators. Neither then nor now does merely coming to the conclusion that the nation is corrupt lead one down the avenue of agencyless spectatorship.

There are many possible actions organizations could take when they are convinced that the system is corrupt, only one of which is dropping out and becoming an observer. It is true that many did follow that road. Especially during the period in question, however, far more chose other options. Some became active reformers—Rorty's preferred route. Others tried to change the system at its most fundamental level. We can argue about which path was better, although King and Malcolm X thought they needed each other, each believing that the system needed to be pressured from multiple directions.

Due to the fallacies in their historical analyses, Gitlin and Rorty were not able to see black radicalism, let alone the broader black community, as an important and critical resource for building a movement capable of addressing global economic woes and other injustices. Rorty, like Gitlin, could not see a way out of the false history that they wrote.

In summary, no matter how sympathetic the treatment, the problems are the same across these various critiques of the black power movement:

1. Misidentification of the nature of the movement, based on incorrect and occasionally blatantly false renditions of the history of the period (Gitlin 1995; Rorty 1998; Brubaker and Cooper 2000).
2. Ascribing a false coherence to an ideologically heterogeneous movement. Often sections of the movement that were not terribly important caused trauma to progressive, radical, and liberal whites and thus became stand-ins for the movement as a whole. Ironically, conservatives and state reactionaries such as J. Edgar Hoover got it right: both the Black Panthers and King *were* dangerous, because they both embodied a transformative black politics dedicated to the redistribution of resources and power to a degree that would have meant a fundamental reconstitution of American society and state.
3. Characterizing the movement as particularistic. In fact, these movements encapsulated the universal, even if the form appeared to the unobservant or stubborn as being particularistic. The Panthers' slogan "National in form, socialist in content" was not just a political statement but an

ontological statement as well. When Brown argued these movements should adopt the language of "I want this for us," she either ignored or was uninformed that this *was* the language of the civil rights movement, of black feminists, of revolutionary black workers, and of revolutionary street organizations such as the Black Panthers, all of whom waged revolution, no matter how unsuccessfully, on behalf of all the oppressed, not just oppressed black people.[3]

A False Universality

A central theme of the critics of the black power movement was that with the move to black power, African Americans switched from organizing based on liberal universal goals and demands—a movement that made demands benefiting all democratic citizens—to a movement organized around the particularistic demands of a single group. Gitlin, for example, berated the white left, which he believed owed its legitimacy to its fight for universal demands, for kowtowing to the black power movement and supporting the particularistic demands of first the black movement and then other movements that emulated the African American model. The New Left was legitimate, according to Gitlin, as long as it embraced "the idea of the Left . . . the belief in the universal community capacity," as its legitimacy "rested on its claim to a place in the grand story of universal human emancipation" (Gitlin 1994, 157–158). According to Gitlin's account, the black-power-fueled rise of identity politics led to both the delegitimization and fragmentation of the left: "The thickening of identity politics is inseparable from the fragmentation of commonality politics. In large measure, things fell apart *because* the center could not hold" (Gitlin 1994, 157). Zerilli summarized this argument in her critique of this point of view: "Universalism is the only alternative to social fragmentation, wild child of the collapse of communism, the rise of deadly nationalism, and the multiculturalist romance with particularism" (Zerilli 1998, 4).

The attacks by Gitlin, Rorty, and similar theorists on the black and allied movements of the 1960s and 1970s echo Bruno Bauer's analysis of the demand for Jewish emancipation in nineteenth-century Europe: "You Jews are *egoists* if you demand a special emancipation for yourselves as Jews. As Germans, you ought to work for the political emancipation of Germany, and as human beings, for the emancipation of mankind, and you should feel the particular kind of your oppression and your shame not as an exception to the rule, but on the contrary as a confirmation of the rule" (Marx 1843, 1). This is the type of logic that substantial segments of the left, as well as many conservatives, have used since the heyday of the Socialist Party to argue that blacks should neither expect nor believe that they have special issues that need to be addressed outside of more central collectivities such as nation, class, gender, or humanity. Bauer went on to ask, "On what grounds, then, do you Jews want emancipation?" (Marx 1843, 2). My answer draws on a history of oppression.

Gitlin is one of the many theorists who incorrectly identify the European and North American left as the embodiment of universal human emancipation. Particularly for leftists, but also for some other radicals as well, the class that embodies the potential for human emancipation, and consequently the focus for the main thrust of leftist organizing, is an idealized working class. Depending on the theorist, the proletariat's pride of place is predicated on

(1) being the most advanced or revolutionary class, (2) being the class most central to the functioning and growth of capitalism, and therefore representing the most strategic class, or (3) being the class that represents the future of all of humanity and therefore the universal class. In sum, fighting for the rights of the working class represented both fighting for all of humanity and fighting for the most advanced sector of the oppressed.

Fredric Jameson's work also echoed Bauer's analysis. In the next chapter I show that Jameson offered much that is useful for contemplating the concept of utopia. In the quote that follows, however, he exhibited the same reductionist, Eurocentric, male-centered view of universalism as the more objectionable work of his fellow theorists. When discussing what type of society could generate worldwide full employment, he provided us with an extraordinary view of oppression that reduces major systems of domination such as the racial order and patriarchy to mere by-products of capitalist failure. This is particularly stunning for someone writing in the first decade of the twenty-first century:

> Crime, war, degraded mass culture, drugs, violence, boredom, the lust for power, the lust for distraction, the lust for nirvana, sexism, racism—all can be diagnosed as so many results of a society unable to accommodate the productiveness of all its citizens. (Jameson 2004, 38)

He later extended this line of analysis:

> We are all shackled to an ideological subject-position, we are all determined by class and class history even when we try to resist or escape it. And for those unfamiliar with this

ideological perspectivism or class standpoint theory, it is perhaps
necessary to add that it holds for everyone, left or right, progressive or reactionary, worker as well as boss, and underclasses,
marginals, ethnic or gender victims, fully as much as for the
ethnic, race or gender mainstreams. (Jameson 2004, 46–47)

For all of the dismissiveness Rorty exhibited toward Jameson on
other issues, they agreed on this point. What Jameson seemed to
miss is that while class may affect us all, it does not mean that
there are not other systems of shackles that are equally binding
and which in some contexts are more powerful at shaping politics
and the social, economic, and psychological terrain within which it
occurs. Economic history and class position are not the only universal forces that operate within modern society. More specifically,
Zerilli argued:

Intersubjective agreement is not there to be discovered in the
universality of experience or the sameness of identity. There
is nothing that we all share by virtue of being human or of
living in a particular community that guarantees a common
view of the world; there is nothing extralinguistic in the
world that guarantees that we all share a common experience;
there is no Archimedean place from which we could accede
to a universalist standpoint. . . . [U]niversality [is] a site of
multiple significations which concern not the singular truths
of classical philosophy but the irreducibly plural standpoints
of democratic politics. (Zerilli 1998, 8)

If Bauer argued, "We must emancipate ourselves before we can
emancipate others" (Marx 1843, 3), Jameson argued equally
incorrectly that liberating oneself liberates others as well. It is only

because class politics in the United States are weak, as Brubaker and Cooper argued, that "we" (the white left) got distracted by "your" movements (identity-politics-based movements, preeminently the black power movement), to the detriment of all.

Many theorists and historians have criticized this viewpoint from multiple angles. One criticism is that the above conception of the "universal" is anything but universal. It is grounded in a European historical experience that privileges the experiences of a relatively narrow segment of toilers. For example, Gitlin's conception of the universal could be argued to fit the following comment by Eduardo Mendieta: "The universality that emerged, however, of the modernity inaugurated with . . . [the] invasion and invention of the Americas has been but the projection of an ethnocentric and deeply devastating rationality" (Mendieta 2003, 16). As Enrique Dussel and Geoff Eley showed, Gitlin, Brubaker and Cooper, and their ilk celebrate a false universality that takes what is a temporally confined and locally grounded working class as standing in for all of humanity—when in fact most of humanity is written out of their histories altogether, or demonized and then dismissed (Dussel 2003; Eley 2007).

The universalism so cherished explicitly by Gitlin and implicitly by Rorty does not appear so universal if we think of the universal in political terms, as political theorists such as Hannah Arendt, Ernesto Laclau, and Linda Zerilli urged us to do. Zerilli made the point that Jameson missed when she argued that theorizing about the universal needs to take into account the existence of multiple contending political claims:

> Any attempt to inscribe the universal will always be confronted and limited by other inscriptions. Politics consists in the mediation of these claims or, as Judith Butler writes,

"how and whether they may be reconciled with one another." It is not a matter of weighing each particular claim to
the universal against some transcultural or transhistorical universal, or of deciding which claim will be authorized as the
"true universal" according to some preexisting normative,
ethical, or cognitive criteria. It is a matter, rather, of mediat-
ing the relation between the particular and the universal in a
public space, with every mediation remaining open to further
mediations. *Rather than think the universal as something that is
extrapolitical and that can be used to adjudicate political claims, we
should think it as a product of political practice.* (Zerilli 1998, 19;
emphasis added)

Further, as Zerilli later intimated, the resistance of Rorty, Gitlin,
and Brubaker and Cooper to considering any other group other
than a particularly narrow segment of the working class as being
able to politically embody the universal implies that people of color
and women "do not have the capacity to represent the universal."
As she went on to argue for the West, whose burden Rorty implicitly assumed in the work I am analyzing, the universal is "little
more than an inflated particular" (Zerilli 2009, 298).

Zerilli built off the work of Laclau, who argued explicitly that
the concept of the universal celebrated by Gitlin and the others is
grounded in nothing more or less than Eurocentric particularism
and Europe's imperialist project:

So, European imperialist expansion had to be presented in
terms of a universal civilizing function, modernization and so
forth. The resistances of other cultures were, as a result, presented not as struggles between particular identities and cul-

tures, but as part of an all-embracing and epochal struggle between universality and particularisms—the notion of peoples without history expressing precisely their incapacity to represent the universal. . . . Some of them [social agents] are going to be privileged agents of historical change, not as a result of a contingent relation of forces but because they are incarnations of the universal. The same type of logic operating in Eurocentrism will establish the ontological privilege of the proletariat. (Laclau 1996, 24–25)

Dussel argued for a different, less Eurocentric understanding of universality, one that acknowledges the rosy dawn of capitalism, and the history of oppression and resistance. In his introduction to Dussel's book Mendieta explained:

Modern philosophy, from Descartes through Hegel and Kant up to Habermas, has labored at projecting a utopian land of universality while covering the historical tracks that have made such an ideal both possible and necessary. By uncovering the historical traces and recovering the material conditions of philosophical production, Dussel has sought to provincialize an alleged universality, thus opening up a way to a transversality, or situated cosmopolitanism, that is attentive to its historical origin but which seeks dialogue across differences. (Mendieta 2003, 14)

Some have argued that oppression makes a reasonable categorical substitute for theorizing the basis of universal claims. In my opinion, oppression is not a full replacement; there probably is no adequate replacement. The concept of oppression is elastic enough to allow us to think about subordination, but one size does not fit all. One has to think through each different system of hierarchy and then use democratic processes to politically resolve the differences that emerge between competing claims. Yet Laclau argues that no particular group can stand for the universal in all places and at all times. Seyla Benhabib made the same point with respect to Marxism when she argued:

> Marx proceeded from the model of a demiurge-like humanity externalizing itself through its own activity in history and yet facing its own externalized capacities as "capital," as the sum total of those alien forces that oppress individuals. Emancipation signified that this alienated potential would be reappropriated by individuals themselves. Here Marx committed a distributive fallacy. He assumed that since humanity as an empirical subject was one, humanity qua normative subject could be represented by *one* particular group. (Benhabib 1986, 351)

As Laclau made clear, however, the fact that no particular group need stand for the universal (whether the group is part of a dominant hegemonic regime or a challenger such as the proletariat) does not mean that every group has an equal chance or claim to that status. First, just because social structure is not determinate does not mean that it is irrelevant (Laclau 1996, 1990). Second, and just as important, it is through political contestation—as Zerilli (1998) emphasized—that various groups make their claim for universality. How one might adjudicate those claims is considered in the next section.

Black Liberation and New Notions
of Universality

> *Here we have a dialectical* materialist *connection, where the*
> *particular neglect of black women leads to the obstruction of the*
> *universal (anti-imperialism and class struggle).*
> —CAROLE DAVIES, DESCRIBING CLAUDIA JONES'S THEORETICAL
>   ARGUMENT ABOUT WHY COMMUNISTS SHOULD EMBRACE THE
>   STRUGGLE OF BLACK WOMEN

On what basis can the black movements of the 1960s and 1970s
be understood as grounded in the universal? As Zerilli and others
suggested, such claims must be considered politically. Following
Badiou, if there is to be a new universality, unlike the previous
leftist incarnation that was inscribed into a narrow segment of the
Euro-American working class, it must "not present itself under
the aspect of a particularity" (Badiou 2003, 99). The contested,
politically constituted identities for groups such as blacks and
women that Zerilli (1998) called for would require (as Badiou
argues in his analysis of Paul's gospels) that blacks be "resubjecti-
vated" such that it is also true for black movements for justice that
"in you shall all the nations be blessed" (Badiou 2003, 103). Thus
in Badiou's terms, black progressive movements would be a site of
universalism. This was the goal envisioned by Guinier and Torres
when they proposed their political race project: "Political race
seeks to construct a new language to discuss race, in order to rebuild a progressive democratic movement led by people of color
but joined by others. The political dimension of the political race
project seeks to reconnect individual experiences to democratic
faith" (Guinier and Torres 2002, 12). The particular—in this case,
the particularity of race—politically stands for and embraces the

universal, in that success for this political project entails that all structures of domination and injustice be dismantled.

By concentrating on the political, we begin to recover a universalism that not only respects but is built on a recognition of the particular. Intersubjective agreements are achieved not through the recognition of some essentialist, ahistorical, transcendental category but through engaging in common political projects, through intermovement negotiations and conflict, through the forging of practices out of which develops a new language of politics. According to Zerilli, we need to "develop just this political idiom in which to rearticulate the relation between universality and particularity, an idiom that eschews truth criteria (and rule following) in favor of opinions formed through contingent practices of publicity. In this idiom the potential moments of intersubjective agreement are anticipated in the context of plurality rather than derived from some notion of an essential commonality or the injunction to reach consensus" (Zerilli 1998, 7).

In contrast, Rorty and Gitlin failed to recognize that their own "communitarian particularisms" prevented their access to the universal as well as blocked their ability to recognize the universalist impulses within the radical wings of what they considered to be disastrous identity-based movements (Badiou 2003, 108). Moishe Postone suggested a methodology by which one may attempt to ascertain the content of universality in a given historical context. He argued that the specific analysis of a given historical terrain is necessary:

> The centrality of proletarian labor to Marx's analysis of capitalism should not be taken as an affirmative evaluation on his part of its ontological primacy to social life, or as part of an

argument that workers are the most oppressed group in society. (Postone 1993, 356 n. 120)

Thus we need to implement an analysis that

> allows one to investigate the relation of various critical conceptions and practices to their historical context—in terms of the constitution of such conceptions and practices, as well as in terms of their possible historical effects—and thereby allows one to consider the role such oppositional subjectivity and practices might play in relation to the possible negation of capitalism. In short, such an approach allows one to analyze the possibility that the existing order might be transformed. (Postone 1993, 38)

Necessarily, I start with the view that in order to imagine new, just societies we must follow the process described by Erik Olin Wright when he argues we must attack the challenges to human flourishing that

> include structures of power and privilege linked to gender, race, ethnicity, sexuality, nationality, and citizenship. The idea of envisioning real utopias, therefore, must ultimately include an account of institutional arrangements for robust egalitarianism in all off these dimensions. Nevertheless, since capitalism so pervasively and powerful structures the prospects of establishing both egalitarian conditions for human flourishing and democratic empowerment, any radical democratic egalitarian project of social transformation must come to terms with the

nature of capitalism and the prospect for this transformation. (Wright 2010, 33)

I agree with Wright's analysis, but intersecting structures of power also suggest the contours of structures of privilege differ by locale, and relatedly, that therefore, oppositional movements also could differ from place to place depending on the nature of local patterns of intersectionality. I am more skeptical of Wright's claim that capitalism is corrosive of ascriptive inequalities "at least in competitive labor markets" (Wright 2010, 46). The historical record suggests that this corrosive process within the United States is one that is quite slow. Capitalism is amazingly adaptive particularly when it comes to *reinforcing* modes of inequality.

Panitch and Gindin also emphasize the need for taking context into consideration when analyzing structures of privilege and power, and the need to study the actual choices actors made, historical paths followed, and analyze actual institutions. I agree with this approach, but note that if we take seriously the need for contextualization then we must also analyze how these phenomena interact with other constitutive hierarchical orders—in the United States this means taking an intersectional approach that includes the study of race, gender, and class. One cannot understand American capitalism, either historically or in its current configuration, without understanding the profound role that the racial order has had in shaping capitalism in the United States, key institutions such as markets, and the state itself. Clearly, capitalism has also shaped the racial order, but it is a two-way street and all too often the absence of an analysis of race has led to dire consequences theoretically and politically. One example of their incomplete analysis is demonstrated when they argue, "One key feature of this transformation was the deeper incorporation of the American working class despite its considerable militancy immediately after World War II" (Panitch and Gindin 2012, Kindle location 362). But as they later state, the black working class was not incorporated, even partially, until decades later and not fully then. The same was true with women's work in and outside of the home. Indeed black radical political economists such as James Boggs and Abram Harris have argued persuasively that it was the super exploitation of black workers that made possible the incorporation of white males into the economy, as did colonial labor exploitation and resource extraction enable the increased integration of workers in the metropole countries (Boggs 1970; Darrity 1989). A gender analysis would yield similar, not identical, results as the mode of economic exploitation for women in general differed from that of the black workforce—although it should be noted black women often experienced exploitation both as women and blacks. To understand the transformative and universal potential of black or other movements requires then analysis of both the structures of power and the political content of those movements.

An analysis of black movements in the United States during the 1960s and 1970s would lead to the following conclusions. Black liberation movements, including those of the 1960s and 1970s, traditionally have been centered on the concepts of freedom, self-determination, and economic justice. I have argued throughout these chapters that the last can be fairly easily reconciled with leftist understandings of the universal; the first two dimensions can also be so reconciled. The struggle *for* freedom can be conceived, following Pettit (1997), as a struggle *against* domination. An important aspect of the struggle against domination, according to Pettit, is freedom from arbitrary interference.

The prototypical case for him is the master-slave relationship. But many evils of black subordination also came under this rubric, such as blacks' status under Jim Crow, when any white person in the South could arbitrarily put at risk the life of any black person, or in our time the often arbitrary and unjust harassment of young black men by the police. When the black freedom struggle is seen in this light, we can also better understand the grounding for the demand for self-determination. The demand for self-determination is in essence a demand for self-rule—a demand aimed squarely at eliminating unjust domination of African Americans in the social, political, cultural, and economic arenas. Indeed, then, black civil society and its associated publics should be seen as a positive good in that historically they have been sites where blacks have been able to operate politically with a fair degree of autonomy, relatively free of domination.[4] Thus black movements' struggle for freedom, self-determination, and economic justice can be seen as being squarely aimed at dismantling systems of subordination, domination, and oppression, all of which are central obstructions to human emancipation in the United States.

It is also true that there were tactical reasons that the demand for self-determination grew to prominence during the twentieth century. As recounted in the last chapter, black activists often were frustrated in their attempts to find reliable white allies. Boggs argued that there was a materialist reason for the lack of working-class unity: "The slogan 'black and white, unite and fight,' which is explicitly or implicitly accepted by so many liberals and radicals, is based on the erroneous idea that there has been a working-class unity between the races in North American history. The fact is that the white workers have been gaining at the expense of the Negroes for so long that for them to unite with the Negroes would be like cutting their own throats" (Boggs 1970, 10). This perception of the failure of multiracial movements to win over working-class whites provided another justification for the demand for self-determination. The demand was also viewed as a necessary response to hostility within the ranks of the working class—not a fantasy generated out of an identity-politics-based movement.[5]

Tommie Shelby quoted Du Bois as presenting a view of black identity founded on the universal political task of struggling for a democratic America—one that is deeply rooted in black political thought: "We believe it is the duty of the Americans of Negro descent, as a body, to maintain their race identity until this mission of the Negro people is accomplished, and the ideal of human brotherhood has become a practical possibility" (Shelby 2002, 235). Black revolutionaries of the black power era sharpened Du Bois's view by focusing less on identity and more on the content of black movements for justice. Boggs argued that black-power-era movements transcended the particular precisely because of the need to dismantle the overall system of domination in order to win black demands: "That is why the black revolution, even though it is not an all-American revolution in the sense that it involves all the Americans who are oppressed, is still an American revolution in the sense that it threatens to wreck the whole system by which the United States has operated" (Boggs 1970, 12). Seven years later, during the height of the black power movement, Boggs further sharpened his argument and demonstrated why the black power movement must see as its tasks taking on all the systems of domination and, in his view, oppressions that bedeviled subordinated groups within the United States. According to Boggs, the black power movement was part of a movement for complete human emancipation:

Nor is it possible for blacks to free themselves without turning over every institution of this society. The Black Power movement must recognize that if this society is ever going to be changed to meet the needs of black people, then Black Power will have to resolve the problems of the society as a whole and not just those of black people. In other words, Black Power cannot evade tackling all the problems of this society, because at the root of all the problems of black people is the same structure and the same system which is at the root of all the problems of all people. (Boggs 1970, 173)

This view was a source of contention within the black power movement, but as Boggs himself argued, the Black Panther Party was an indicator, no matter how imperfect, that the movement was heading in the right direction. It was becoming a movement that, while fighting for black liberation, understood that this could be accomplished only by taking on the burden of leading a broad movement that would dismantle all systems of oppression. This issue led to the murder of two Panthers at the University of California, Los Angeles, by cultural nationalists, but in the end this was the ideological tendency that was most strongly supported by the black grass roots—and it was a goal that could be said to stand for the universal, as theoretically suggested by Zerilli, Postone, and Laclau.

With the critical exception of King during his later years, in some ways the black power movement was in aspiration if not in practice more transformative than the mainstream civil rights movement. Multiple wings of the movement were more explicitly anticapitalist, more explicitly allied with other movements both domestic and international, more convinced that the only way to black liberation involved the dismantling of the multiple structures of domination with which African Americans had been forced to contend. Tactically, there were enormous differences between the black power and civil rights movements, as there were enormous differences in tone, but both movements were heterogeneous and had very strong progressive wings. Neither movement should be conceived as being primarily based on identity politics, and identity politics was not the reason that the left and progressive movements of the 1970s collapsed. The civil rights and black power movements made demands that at their root entailed the revolutionary transformation not only of American society but of capitalism itself. Consequently, both fulfilled the prerequisites that could have led to a reversal of the sundering and an articulation of movements that, particularly in alliance with the other insurgencies of the time, would have allowed them to stand in for a universal, as it had become clear that the classically conceived proletariat could no longer fulfill that role.[6] Yet neither the black power movement nor the civil rights movement (nor yet the women's movement, which in a different manner could be argued to have similar potential) ultimately succeeded in becoming encompassing enough to be able to take the next step and serve as the basis of a transformative movement that would fundamentally reshape not only civil society and to some degree the racial order but the economic system as well.

So What Did Kill the Radical Movement?

So what did kill the radical movement?

There are several factors: political, demographic, moral, and coercive forces all played a role. A significant amount of the responsibility for the left's decline rests with the movement itself. One of these self-inflicted wounds came with the transition of many predominantly nonwhite revolutionary groups into the New Communist movement. As Alain Badiou argued with respect to the French (particularly Maoist) left of the same period, American revolutionaries were trying to find an answer to "the most difficult question [which] is probably what type of organization we need" (Badiou 2010, 65). For different reasons than in France, the New Communist movement in the United States was a failure. An absolutely fatal consequence of this move was the movement-wide decision to pull activists out of organizing—in workplaces, in the community, in artistic endeavors, and on college campuses—in order to do the theoretical and organizational work necessary for party building. This cut off from its base what had been one of the most solidly entrenched grassroots movements—which means it was cut off from material and political support, from new recruits, from new ideas, from any sense of reality. In the U.S. left and black radical movements "theory was excessively overvalued" as Harnecker argued it was in the Latin American left (Harnecker 2007, 52). Further, theory building among radicals was actually not real theory building in the sense in which it occurs in the social and natural sciences, where theories can be tested and, if necessary, revised or scrapped. Rather, it was ill-disguised uncritical faith—not the faith of a Cornel West or a Martin Luther King Jr., based on a probing, engaged intellect open to new ideas and opportunities, but rather the faith of the ministers that King addressed in his "Letter from a Birmingham Jail," those whose narrow-minded ideology was justified by the use of scripture, with the result that they had closed their hearts and minds to progressive, loving (to use King's language) possibilities for the democratic transformation of the segregated South (King 1986c). The same errors were made by many radicals who certainly closed their minds and often their hearts, even if the scripture in this case was very different, by refusing to consider alternative interpretations, paths, and theory.

The turn to Maoism and other forms of Leninism by the American left led to the repeat of many of the same mistakes that the CPUSA made during the first half of the twentieth century. One of these mistakes was embracing a romanticized portrait of a regime that initially may have assisted in overthrowing a brutal government oppressing those at the bottom of society, but which soon proved brutal and antidemocratic itself. Yet the left took its cues for morality from sources that all too often were utterly corrupt and antidemocratic. This led American Maoists, for example, in the second period of black insurgency to take morally indefensible positions (such as not supporting the African National Congress in South Africa because the Chinese supported a different faction; supporting the Cultural Revolution and ignoring its brutality and the harm it did to the Chinese people; or for the case of some black nationalists, supporting the regime of Idi Amin in Uganda in the name of black nationalism).

The turn to Maoism deserves to be probed in more depth. There were significant differences between Maoism and earlier Leninist variants that shaped not just the New Communist movement (which partly evolved out of the major white leftist antiwar organization, Students for a Democratic Society) but also the black radicalism (both revolutionary nationalist and black leftist) of the 1960s and 1970s.[7] The turn to Maoism not only played a major part in defining the differences between the two periods of black radicalism but also directly contributed to the decline of black radicalism and the left.[8]

A key attraction of Maoism for second-period black radicals was the symbolic political support and attention the black movement received from the Chinese Communist Party (CCP). For example, in 1963, three weeks before the March on Washington, Mao Zedong made the following statement: "The evil system of colonialism and imperialism arose and throve with the enslavement of Negroes and the trade in Negroes, and it will surely come to its end with the complete emancipation of the black people" (Kelley and Esch 1999, 9). This stands in stark contrast to the stance of the CPUSA, which was downplaying the civil rights movement and, as we saw, attacked black nationalism in all of its forms. It is not a coincidence that the first of the major third-path organizations to develop during this second period, the Revolutionary Action Movement (RAM), was attracted to Maoism and defined its revolutionary nationalist program in the early 1960s in a manner adopted later in the decade by organizations such as the Black Panther Party and the League of Revolutionary Black Workers. RAM, formed in the early 1960s and building off the work of Harold Cruse, "represented the first serious and sustained attempt in the postwar period to wed Marxism, black nationalism, and Third World internationalism into a coherent revolutionary program" (Kelley and Esch 1999, 14). The group received mentoring and inspiration from first-period black Marxists who had been purged from the CPUSA as well as those more influenced by the Trotskyite left, such as James and Grace Lee Boggs. As Kelley and Esch documented, RAM made the classic third-path claim—a claim black leftists made both inside and outside Marxist organizations—when it argued that black nationalism "is really internationalism" (Kelley and Esch 1999, 19).

A related aspect of Maoism that the black left found attractive was that, unlike other forms of Marxism and Leninism, it was not considered Eurocentric. As the Black Panther Party's minister of information, Eldridge Cleaver, stated, "Comrade Mao Tse-Tung applied the classical principles of Marxism-Leninism to the conditions of [his] own countr[y] and thereby made the ideology into something useful for [his] people. But [he] rejected that part of the analysis that was not beneficial to them and had only to do with the welfare of Europe" (Kelley and Esch 1999, 14). Kelley and Esch argued that this attractiveness for black radicals was enhanced by the CCP's willingness to stand up to the West with force.

A key aspect of black radicalism, according to Kelley and Esch—and again they were absolutely on the mark—was the realization that "cultural activism and political activism are not two different strategies for liberation but two sides of the same coin. The cultural revolution and the political revolution go hand in hand" (Kelley and Esch 1999, 34). Amiri Baraka and the Revolutionary Communist League (RCL) were instrumental in bringing the black arts movement into black radicalism and particularly black leftist organizing. Unlike other former black nationalist organizations, the RCL (previously known as the Congress of African People) did *not* downgrade cultural work once it evolved into a communist organization. It was distinctive in large part because, "more than any other Maoist or anti-revisionist, Baraka and the RCL epitomized the most conscious and sustained effort to bring the Great Proletarian Cultural Revolution [revolutionary art and culture] to the inner cities of the United States" (Kelley and Esch 1999, 35). More generally in the realm of culture, Maoism was attractive, Kelley and Esch argued, because "Maoism's emphasis on revolutionary ethics and moral transformation, in theory at least, resonated with black religious traditions" (Kelley and Esch 1999, 18).

Philosophically, Maoism's emphasis on practice being a key foundation for knowledge and theory was an appealing feature for second-period black nationalists. As Kelley and Esch detailed, "Central to Maoism is the idea that Marxism can be (must be) reshaped to the requirements of time and place and that practical work, ideas, and leadership stem from the masses in movement not from a theory created in the abstract or produced out of other struggles" (Kelley and Esch 1999, 9). This had the positive effect of empowering both cadres and grassroots organizers to challenge "experts" who often were more concerned with containing black movements than with attacking the underlying causes of black disadvantage and subordination. Generally, Maoist organizations (and other black radical organizations of the period) invested enormous energy and resources in consciousness-raising activities such as running bookstores, establishing study groups, distributing propaganda, putting out frequent and regular newspapers, producing endless pamphlets, and designing actions with the express intent to educate the masses. Kelley and Esch argued that this work had a deeper purpose than perhaps a surface examination would produce: "But consciousness raising was more than propaganda work; it was intellectual labor in the context of revolutionary practice" (Kelley and Esch 1999, 39). At the height of the movement, black radicals effectively used propaganda and agitation (to use the old communist phrase) to spread a black revolutionary analysis of the roots of what they viewed as black oppression and to provide a road map for black liberation.

Another of the old left's mistakes that was repeated by American leftists of the later generation was that they did not seriously analyze conditions within the United States and use their own experience and understanding of those conditions to formulate theory and strategy, instead mechanically applying models from outside the United States. I want to emphasize that black leftism, and to some degree certain black nationalisms, shared this fatal flaw with the rest of American leftism, relying on foreign models for both moral and political guidance. Whether one is thinking of Marxism, Maoism, or influential writings from the radical black diaspora such as those of Frantz Fanon, Julius Nyerere, Kwame Nkrumah, Amilcar Cabral, or Aimé Césaire, it is clear that no political analysis could be mechanically applied to an extraordinarily powerful capitalist country that was also profoundly shaped by a racial order. The best of these writers emphasized that analysis needed to start with conditions within a specific country, history, and culture. For example, radicals of all stripes, not just the liberals Guinier justifiably excoriated, failed to analyze how racial desegregation affected white workers and the white lower middle class. The white upper middle class could and did buy themselves out of desegregation by using market mechanisms to create racially (and class) exclusive enclaves and institutions. According to Guinier, "Many working-class and poor whites had acquired an investment in white privilege. . . . Not surprisingly, remedies involving desegregation evoked virulent hostility among such whites" (Guinier 2004, 92). Neither the investment in white privilege nor the virulent reaction was seriously analyzed and factored into strategies to bring disadvantaged whites into coalitions with nonwhite populations they often viewed as both culturally reprehensible and materially the source of their troubles. This failure would fuel conservative electoral successes for the next forty years as well as the general rightward shift of politics in the United States. Further, Kelley and Esch were absolutely right when they argued that the black left did not take to heart some of Mao's key dictums. Revolutionary struggle is protracted. It is not for the impatient. Like those of other faiths and creeds who anticipate imminent salvation, black and other radicals had no backup strategy for when things went bad and it became clear that revolutionary success was not immediately forthcoming. This failing was compounded by the lack of clear analysis and understanding of the rapidly changing nature of politics, society, and economy in the United States.

Another form of self-inflicted wound was the misogyny that often ran rampant within the various progressive movements, including the civil rights, black nationalist, and black leftist wings. Multiple forms of masculinism were practiced within movement organizations. While the Black Panthers did not invent thug life, they practiced, organizationally institutionalized, and theoretically justified it to unprecedented heights. The Panthers did some incredibly important work, including the work of the so-called reformist side after the split, but it was undermined by a brutal sexism within the organization itself. As historians of the black insurgency as well as the black feminists of the times have extensively documented, the Black Panthers were not an isolated case; sexism undermined work and oppressed women throughout all wings of the movement. However, I partially disagree with Kelley and Esch's argument that Mao's dictum "Women hold up half the sky" provided some theoretical cover for women cadres fighting misogyny and patriarchy within black radicalism despite the deeply problematic practices of the CCP on gender (Kelley and Esch 1999). While I believe this is to some degree true, what was more dominant was the CCP's explicitly homophobic views and practices, and the lack of traction that gender equality had within the black left during the 1960s and 1970s. Indeed, Kelley has written on the generally masculinist and patriarchal understanding of the proletariat and proletarian revolution found within the U.S. communist movement. That tendency, combined with the ultra-masculinism and militarism promoted by significant segments of black radicalism—nationalist and Marxist alike—more often than not led to the principle of gender equality within organizations being given lip service at best. The misogyny in all sectors of the left proved to be a key contributing factor to the decline of the U.S. left—a factor to which Maoism substantially contributed.

Just as Maoist organizations did not prove at all immune to the sexism that pervaded the left, these organizations also proved not to be immune to the tendency of Marxist organizations of all stripes to belittle the importance of black movements and attack black nationalism in all of its myriad forms. The Progressive Labor Party (PLP), one of the first Maoist organizations, was typical of some Maoist organizations that acted like the early twentieth-century Socialist Party. As Kelley and Esch noted, "The PLP's relationship with black community activists . . . [was] damaged in part because of its attack on the Black Panther Party and the black student movement" (Kelley and Esch 1999, 11). Years later, one of the critical mistakes that Huey Newton's wing of the Black Panther Party made during the early 1970s was traveling the same path the CPUSA and PLP had gone down several years earlier—abandoning the core political demand of the black movement, which was self-determination, claiming that changes in the American economy no longer made such a demand necessary. Later in the decade many of the New Communist organizations that emerged out of the black, Chicano, Puerto Rican, and Asian American radical movements started to seriously deemphasize the central role that black liberation could play in transforming society while increasing attacks on black nationalists. The goal of a unified CPUSA-like organization was never achieved during the latter part of the second period, and eventually most of these organizations no longer could be classified as third-path organizations because they had become more and more doctrinaire, albeit Maoist.

With the abandonment of the third path during the transition to the New Communist movement, once again black and other leftists began downplaying the role of work among blacks and other subordinate racial and ethnic groups on issues of justice. Combined with the retreat from grassroots organizing, this shift in emphasis cut the progressive wings of the black insurgency off from their strongest bases of support.

Rising rates of immigration led to substantial changes in the Asian American and Latino populations. These changes meant that, going forward into the 1970s and beyond, activists from these communities had less familiarity and fewer working relationships with black activists. The breakdown of cooperation between these groups led to particularly explosive situations in California. In California and elsewhere these tensions were exacerbated by leaders from each of these communities who saw ethnic tension and race baiting as a mechanism for furthering their own careers, increasing their personal power, and garnering significant material resources.

The lack of democracy in all wings of the movement (including substantial segments of the civil rights movement)—a gap between theory and practice—was another source of the decline of radical movements. I want to emphasize two points in particular in regard to this. First, many anticolonial and anti-neocolonial projects have driven home the point that one cannot build democratic societies and states when one's entire struggle is organizationally centered on practices, processes, institutions, and norms that are the antithesis of democratic. Again, this was a problem not just with the left but also with nationalist formations, and to a significant degree with the civil rights movement as well.[9] Second, the curtailment of democracy within liberal and radical movements removes key opportunities for experimentation. Whether our faith is secular or religious, we cannot know the future, nor can we be sure that we have any of the right answers. As social and natural scientists will say, organizations and species that have the potential for experimentation built in have sounder futures on average than those that do not exhibit flexibility.

The violent and coercive efforts of the state are probably the best-documented cause for the rapid decline of the left. From the attempted undermining of the civil rights movement and particularly Martin Luther King Jr. by J. Edgar Hoover's FBI to the police murder of Chicago Black Panther leader Fred Hampton in 1969, the systematic dismantling of the Black Panther Party, and the widespread activities of the FBI's COINTELPRO counterinsurgency program (aimed primarily but not exclusively at black insurgency), massive damage was done to radical movements by the state. The scope of these activities is still not well known even by those active at the time (Button 1978).

All of these factors led to both demoralization and burnout among movement activists. Bryan Palmer's description of the end of the era of Atlantic insurgency at the close of the eighteenth century and the beginning of the nineteenth well describes the sense of despair and its deadly consequences for some activists on this side of the Atlantic 170 years later: "It was the sorry suppression of the dark desire of a long, hard night of unrelieved repression. In the Despard conspiracy Jacobinism sank in a rough sea of unreality, driven to extremist exasperation by a climate of coercion and cold, implacable power" (Palmer 2000, 119).

Conclusion

I spent a substantial amount of time in this chapter discussing why the left disintegrated, focusing particularly on the arguments of Todd Gitlin and his many fellow travelers and criticizing their view that identity politics not only destroyed the left but also fragmented in practice as well as theoretically any sense of the universal, the common good, that they argued had been at the heart of Western radicalism in both its liberal and socialist variants. I pointed out that many theorists (such as radical philosopher and liberation theologist Enrique Dussel) and historians (such as Geoff Eley) have already done much of the spadework necessary to undermine the privileged place of Western conceptions of the "universal." I acknowledged the difficulty in reframing or regaining a sufficiently broad and powerful concept of the universal; it may not be possible to do so. I do reject Gitlin's notion that the only hope for a new universal movement lies in the environmental movement, as important as that movement is to humanity's future. As William Connolly, the authors who constitute the Retort collective, and others have argued, recent events suggest that anticapitalist movements are being globally constructed but are no longer based on the notion of an industrial proletariat, an outdated idea that never played its theorized role in either the growth of global capitalism or resistance to capitalism. It is quite possible that we are permanently in an era where a number of more or less parallel movements challenge injustice. Or we could follow the lead of philosophers such as Iris Young and turn to the concept of "oppression" as a broader but messier conception of a quasi universal. Malcolm X once said, "The oppressed people of this earth make up a majority, not a minority" (Haywood 1978, 629). This was the practical consensus that black radicals and their allies had reached by the late 1960s. Ending that oppression, many thought at the time, would be the business of the various movements during the 1970s and beyond. It is an uneasier but sounder route to realize that, as Zerilli and Laclau remarked, there is no transhistorical group that can stand in for the universal; an appropriate signifier must be determined in each period by political contestation.

One of the great tragedies that accompanied the shift of black radicals into the New Communist movement of the 1970s was the loss of the combined promise that the civil rights and black power movements once had to stand for a movement so transformative that it had universalist implications for the United States. During the 1960s and early 1970s black movements and their allies within other social movements began to collectively ask what the country would look like if no group was exploited or dominated. As black and other radicals lost or abandoned their ties to their communities, fewer and fewer asked this question, and those who did ask it no longer had an audience, let alone supporters.

A question we are left with is whether black radicalism, weaker than it has been in a century, has any relevance for black politics of the present or future. I argued earlier that public opinion work indicates that the political base for such movements still has strong support. What should be clear from this chapter and the last is that while there are perhaps intriguing lessons to be learned from the earlier periods of black insurgency, a complete break must be made—not with the past of black politics but with the bankrupt practice of not doing the hard work of determining and analyzing potential future paths ourselves.

As we think about the future of black radical politics, what we should strive to regain is a politically constituted definition of "black" that is, to quote Alain Badiou, "less the demand of a social fraction or community to be integrated into the existing order than something which touches on a transformation of the order as a whole" (Badiou 2001, 109).

Chapter 4

Modern Myths

Constructing Visions of the Future

Seize the Time!
—BLACK PANTHER PARTY SLOGAN, CIRCA 1970

It does not matter who killed the left, does it? Because we live in a postracial society.

Dinesh D'Souza, the author of the 1995 book *The End of Racism,* is one of a gaggle of conservative pundits who found the silver lining of a postracial society in what was for them the otherwise devastating victory of Barack Obama in the 2008 U.S. presidential election. He commented after Obama's victory: "If Obama's election means anything, it means that we are now living in postracist America. That's why even those of us who didn't vote for Obama have good reason to celebrate" (D'Souza 2009).

In *Not in Our Lifetimes* (Dawson 2011) I describe in detail how the Obama campaign was many things to many people—including a substantial number of Americans hoping for a truly transformative moment, one that would see the rebirth of decency, hope for a decent life for ordinary people, the rebuilding of progressive, antiracist politics, and the resurrection of democracy in America. These were the genuine aspirations of the millions of people of all races, but particularly nonwhite Americans and youth of all races, who mobilized in unprecedented numbers to campaign for Barack Obama. More than anything else, however, I argued, the campaign was a spectacle, a cynical manipulation of what potentially was a moment of transformative politics. The missed opportunity led to the papering over of real cleavages of race and class, promotion of a false national unity (public opinion data from the time decisively demonstrate the deep divisions within the electorate even at the time of Obama's greatest popularity), and the embracing of a political amnesia that denied the sins of racial subordination and disadvantage in both past and present.[1]

What the election of Barack Obama as president of the United States *did not* signify was the advent of a postracial society. One of the seductive fallacies advanced to argue that we live in a postracial society is that with the victories of the civil rights movement and the formal dismantling of state apartheid—truly a brilliant victory for democracy in America—blacks were completely emancipated. Martin Luther King Jr.'s mountain had been climbed, the banners could be furled, and we could get on with the task of building an America that, if not yet fully free of racial prejudice, at least was free of the formal, structural barriers of racial disadvantage. Barack Obama's election was just another, brilliant symbol of our success in breaking apart the structures of racism. Racism was relegated to the province of individual prejudice, and Obama's election showed once again how little force prejudice actually exerted in American politics and society.[2]

At the end of his life King clearly did not believe that the victories of the civil rights movement had ushered in a new postracial era. Marx's insights in "On the Jewish Question" help us understand why the true victories of the civil rights movement did not mark the advent of an era of full black emancipation. The same logic that Marx used to argue that political emancipation led to incomplete religious emancipation can be concretely applied to the status of blacks: the political emancipation that was a consequence of the dismantling of Jim Crow did nothing to prevent racism from flourishing in civil society, including in markets.

Marx wrote, "It is possible, therefore, for the *state* to have emancipated itself from religion even if the *overwhelming majority* is still religious. And the overwhelming majority does not cease to be religious through being religious in private" (Marx 1843, 7). While political emancipation was an important democratic step forward, it is still only one aspect of complete human emancipation.

Just as the "annulment of private property not only fails to abolish private property but even presupposes it" (Marx 1843, 8), the exclusion of race from state processes and regulations does not abolish the force of race in American society; rather, it presupposes it. For Marx, civil society is the locus within the bourgeois democratic state where forces such as religion, property, and (in our case) race operate. And the depoliticization of religion that Marx said occurred when civil society became the locus of religion has its parallel in the post-civil-rights era with the massive depoliticization of issues of race in the United States once the state ceased to be the primary focus of conflict over racial subordination. Indeed, a major focus of white backlash is to further remove the state from adjudicating and regulating affairs involving race. A major difference between how Marx argued religion operated in nineteenth-century Europe and how race operates in the United States today is that religion went from being the basis for community to being the mark of difference, while, as Judith Shklar (1991) pointed out, race in the United States always denoted difference. More precisely, as Thomas Jefferson (1999) made clear, the political community of the United States was founded on racially based political exclusion—the exclusion of blacks from both the political community and civil society. The racial state divides human citizens from a dangerous subhuman, noncitizen population. As King once asked, where do we go from here?

In this chapter I discuss the constraints that the current neoliberal order has imposed on our collective ability not only to forge a democratic politics but even to imagine alternatives to the way we currently live. And I argue that we need the concept of "utopia" in order to reimagine rebuilding black politics and more generally a democratic politics within the United States.

The Impact of Neoliberalism

Marx argued in Volume 1 of *Capital* that capitalism "makes an accumulation of misery a necessary condition, corresponding to the accumulation of wealth. Accumulation of wealth at one pole is, therefore, at the same time accumulation of misery, the torment of labour, slavery, ignorance, brutalization and moral degradation at the opposite pole, i.e. on the side of the class that produces its own product as capital" (Marx 1976, 799). This is a particularly good description of life at the bottom during the capitalist era in which we now live.

The fiction of a good life for most of the working and middle classes becomes impossible to sustain as the responsibility of governments toward their citizens dwindles and the rapaciousness of transnational corporations and the superrich grows without limit. Factory jobs, government positions, and other unionized jobs that once ensured a decent life for a relatively broad sector of Americans have all but disappeared, and the few remaining bastions of unionization are under savage attack. In their place are a wide range of dreary temporary jobs, service economy employment, and the jobs that are often so brutal, dulling, and dangerous that day laborers or migrant workers are the only ones willing to take them on. Between 2007 and 2008 households in the United States lost 22 percent of their net worth (Panitch and Gindin 2012). As Panitch and Gindin argue, one would think that such a precipitous decline in so many people's fortune would provide a "fertile ground" for challenging the current social order. Yet for all too many survival can be an untenable proposition, as Barbara Ehrenreich (2008) shows us, when one *works* at the low end of the labor force. Lauren Berlant describes the consequences of life at the bottom of the neoliberal order: "An all too present cause of the effects . . . is the volatile here and now of that porous domain of hyperexploitative entrepreneurial atomism that has been variously dubbed globalization, liberal sovereignty, late capitalism, post-Fordism, or neoliberalism. It is a scene of mass but not collective activity. It is a scene in which the lower you are on economic scales, and the less formal your relation to the economy, the more alone you are in the project of maintaining and reproducing life. Communities, when they exist, are at best fragile and contingent" (Berlant 2007, 280). Civil society and community are hardly resources for the "solitary agents" at the bottom of the economic order trying every day to survive (Berlant 2007, 282).

These insights are even more forcefully brought home by Sudhir Venkatesh's (2006) ethnography of very poor black communities in the 1990s. As Venkatesh so grimly describes, the very poor, those who must hustle every day to merely survive, and even those who are doing a little better but live in these communities must be constantly attuned to the art of surviving hostile streets where prospects are dim and where society and state prove daily they do not care. Under such conditions they have precious little time or any other resource to devote to politics. The struggle to survive is a full-time preoccupation; there is virtually no time or opportunity for life-affirming activities. This state of affairs is a logical, if not natural, consequence when a society is governed by the principles of a "neoliberalism [that] specifically enshrines capital as the sovereign force in the organizing of society" (Eley 2007, 173).

Dystopian Times

Ideological machinations are needed to encourage political quietude among those most disadvantaged by this society over and above the structurally imposed constraints of bad times. Pushed hard enough, people tend to push back. It is easier to avoid that situation if people believe that either their desperate situation is their own fault or, even if the system is to blame, there is no viable political recourse. For example, blacks and whites generally have different narratives about why some live in such poor conditions. There were two studies of blacks and whites in the Northeast during the 1970s, one a set of in-depth interviews conducted by a political scientist among a number of whites, including poor white Americans, the other conducted by an anthropologist among working-class and lower-middle-class African Americans. What is interesting about the responses from the two studies is that although the region and economic status of the respondents are roughly comparable and the studies were done at around the same time, the black respondents tended to blame the system for poor economic outcomes, while white respondents were more likely to base their attributions of inequality on ideas of individual worth and effort. Quotes drawn from the two studies are illustrative of the differences in black and white attributions of poverty:

> There are two kinds of whitefolks. A few live like they want to and the rest try to live like their big boss leaders. (Sims Patrick, quoted in Gwaltney 1980, 110)

> Their big men keep telling them that they can be big, too, if they keeps us little enough, and that's all they need to hear. I have lived in South Carolina, Georgia, Tennessee, Michigan, New York and plenty of other places, and I haven't been any-where where there were not some white people who were just as poor as most of the black people in those places. . . . [M]ost whitefolks have just enough to make them think that they can get what these big shots have. (Ruth Shays, quoted in Gwalt-ney 1980, 36)

In these quotes, the black subjects implicitly blame the "system" for poverty and their or their community's poor condition, and explicitly accuse whites of being guilty of false consciousness. White subjects, on the other hand, consistently identify individ-ual weaknesses and failure as the cause for poverty, and excellence as the cause for success:

> [The rich] they worked for it, why not? You work for it, it's fair. . . . [I]f you deserve it, you deserve it. I don't believe in this equal, all equal. (Maria Pulaski, quoted in Hochschild 1981, 28)

To misquote the movie *The Usual Suspects*, if the devil's best trick is to make one think he doesn't exist, then neoliberalism's best trick is, as Lauren Berlant put it, to enable one to "imagine one-self as a solitary agent who can and must live the good life prom-ised by capitalist culture" (Berlant 2007, 278). Both the propen-sity of the white respondents to look to themselves for answers about shortcomings in their life and the black respondents' belief that white people "are just that way" preclude thinking about better worlds. Actually, the black respondents provide plenty of evidence that they envision better ways of living in a differently organized society, but because they believe white people "are just the way they are," and because they are realists, they see very little hope for changing the world for the better, particularly along economic lines.

Under a neoliberal regime people forget, or do not believe, that there are agents and institutions that are responsible for their often struggling lives. As Bernard Harcourt points out, the U.S. state has created the most massive penal system in the world, with in-carceration rates surpassing all others. And at the very same time that neoliberalism fosters the myth of free and natural markets, the state has enabled institutions such as the Chicago Board of Trade by "facilitat[ing] a state-sanctioned monopoly and empowered the private practices of a small association of brokers and dealers" (Har-court 2011, 151). Yet those on the bottom are told both that the state is too poor to help *them* and that we live in society ordered by free markets where institutions and citizens succeed or not on their own merits. Making the situation worse is that neoliberalism not only encourages people to forget that the devil exists but also convinces them that we are as close as possible to the creation of paradise on earth.

Neoliberalism's Utopian Substitutes

Berlant is one of many who argue that utopian thinking and aspirations, or even the most rudimentary conception of the good
life, good society, and good state, have been undermined by "the
retraction, during the last three decades, of the social democratic
promise of the post World War II period in the US and Europe"
(2011, 3). Not only have our dreams been undermined, according
to Berlant, but for most of us in this society life has become so
precarious, contingent, and trauma-infused that getting by is a real
accomplishment and the discourse that circulates within what
remains of the public sphere is often focused on precisely how to
get by. She quoted Marcuse as saying that people "continue the
struggle for existence in painful, costly and obsolete forms" (2011,
10). What is different about this period is that while this reality is
nothing new to society's poor (and indeed is also descriptive of a
wide swath of the black middle class, as sociologist Bart Landry
reminded us many years ago), middle-class and even upper-middle-
class whites, particularly white males, are now having to come to
grips with this chaotic reality.[3] To encourage business as usual
and dampen the society-wide unease, the agents of neoliberalism
promote the "normal." The normal is like a security blanket, a
refuge from the daily terrors that confront most people as they
just try to make it from day to day.

Individually and as a society, we are suffering from "cruel optimism," to use Berlant's phrase—a state of being marked by "the
condition of maintaining an attachment to a problematic object."
She continued: "But if the cruelty of an attachment is experienced
by someone/some group, even in disavowed fashion, the fear is
that the object/scene of promising itself will defeat the capacity to

have any hope about anything. Often this fear of loss of a sense of optimism as such is unstated and only experienced in a sudden incapacity to manage startling situations" (Berlant 2008, 33). This phenomenon describes our often irrational refusal to abandon aspects of a political, economic, and social system that has badly served the majority of Americans over the past several decades. America is supposed to be great; its highest aspirations are the stuff out of which the American dream is fabricated. For many Americans this dream has not been fulfilled. But we have not been able to break our attachment to this system. One reason, Berlant suggested, is fear of losing an optimistic sense of America, a sense that at one time was at least partially grounded in reality. If the American dream is broken and turning into Malcolm X's "American nightmare" for more than just poor black Americans, what is to replace it as the source of hope for a better future, if not for us, then at least for our progeny? The answer we hear whispered in our ear in the depths of night is "nothing." There is no source of hope to replace the broken dream we have now.

A second problem is that we cannot accurately name either the problem or the solution. Many of the solutions that the twentieth century held on to have been either justifiably disgraced or so perverted in American discourse that an honest, down-to-earth discussion of concepts such as social democracy is nigh impossible outside semiprotected spaces such as the academy. French philosopher Alain Badiou sternly argued that we must reclaim the language of struggle and resistance and resist the tendency toward self-silencing: "We have to try to retain the words of our language, even though we no longer dare to say them out loud. In '68, these were the words that were used by everyone. Now they tell us: 'The world has changed, so you can no longer use those words, and you know that it was the language of illusions and terror.' 'Oh yes we can! And we must!' *The problem is still there,* and that means that we must be able to pronounce those words. It up to us to criticise them, and to give them new meaning" (Badiou 2010, 64).[4] Even as late as the 1970s, both the left and the right were able to imagine alternatives to the current economic and political order. As Erik Olin Wright has argued, "While the right condemned socialism as violating individual rights to private property and unleashing monstrous new forms of state oppression, and the left saw socialism as opening up new vistas of social equality, genuine freedom and the development of human potentials, both believed that a fundamental alternative to capitalism was possible." Yet, it is hard to either name the problem or imagine the alternative to what we have today as "the natural order of things and pessimism has replaced the optimism of the will that Gramsci said would be essential if the world is to be transformed" (Wright 2010, 1).

On the other hand, many of the problems have names attached to them that have the protected status of sacred relics, such as "capitalism." And when it comes to solutions, names such as "democracy" have had their meanings narrowed to such slim, technocratic dimensions that they no longer can provide the basis for discussions of the good life without a massive battle to reclaim their original contentious, radical, and political meanings. Here political science, as Lisa Wedeen has argued, has played a particularly damaging role, as policy makers, non-governmental organizations (NGOs), and those influential inside the Beltway and in international institutions such as the World Bank have adopted the move by some political scientists to limit the meaning of democracy to merely to the act of voting—ruling out all the other components of democratic life, such as active civic participation, accountability, or a vigorous democratic discourse as either meaningless or unmeasurable (and for far too many social scientists, "unmeasurable" is the functional equivalent of "meaningless") (Wedeen 2008).

Throughout both the nineteenth and twentieth centuries African Americans had the relative luxury of being able to rely on a wide range of black ideologies that saw as a central task the naming of both the problem of black oppression and its solution. The attenuation of the black public sphere, the conversion of many black elites to neoliberal ideology, and the defeat or diminution of a wide variety of black progressive movements (nationalist, feminist, social democratic, and those more to the left) have all greatly reduced the ideological resources African Americans have for identifying problems and solutions and for being able to vigorously debate the merits of alternatives. Blacks no longer have anywhere near the ideological resources they had during the last century for productive utopian thinking and debate.

Political depression is one result of this state of affairs. The political and other spectacles that serve as our Roman circuses are necessary to prevent political depression from turning into righteous anger—or at least that is the theory. The state of affairs that led to widespread political depression is also partly, though not wholly, the source of the hope and affection invested in candidate Barack Obama in 2008. Our institutions have failed and there are no strong mass movements, but he stood as one of the few remaining sites for political hope, and more generally hope for the American dream. The danger of the genuine and understandable optimism generated by the 2008 campaign is that "the vague futurities of normative optimism produce small self-interruptions as the utopias of structural inequality. . . . [S]hifts in affective atmosphere are not equal to changing the world" (Berlant 2008, 49). Without such spectacles, it is even more likely we will be trapped in a syndrome within which "the American Dream does not allow a lot of time for curiosity about people it is not convenient or productive to have curiosity about" (Berlant 2008, 37).

Several visions of contemporary life make it more difficult for us to imagine a better world. In one vision, we are told that we live in the best of all possible worlds. We are told this on television, in the movies, and in music videos. We are only some bling and a black (even better than platinum!) American Express card away from the good life to which we all should aspire.

Conversely, a more dystopian vision tells us that there is no good life—that everything has decayed and cannot be recovered; that, as Rousseau and Machiavelli feared and anticipated, modernity corrupts; and that in this neo-Hobbesian world we live in, only the strong survive. The current economic crisis can be read as the extension of black dystopia into the previously perceived, if illusory, good life of middle-class white suburbia. In this view, thinking about better alternatives is a waste of time; all any of us can do is hope that we survive and that our tribe proves to be the strongest.

A third alternative defines the vision of the good life as Pat Buchanan, Glenn Beck, Rush Limbaugh, and their compatriots do. We regain this vision by returning to a mythical version of 1950s America: where black men and all women knew their place; where non-European immigrants were both invisible and silent; where, as Pat Buchanan recently said, white men were properly respected for building all that is good in this country; where queers did not exist, and if they did, they had the common courtesy not to allow their deviance to become public; where democracy was mainly limited to, and power strictly exercised by, those who deserved to rule (Buchanan 2011). In such a world, "foreigners are only tolerable so long as they 'integrate' themselves into the magnificent model presented to them by our institutions, our astonishing systems of education and representation. Proof that, so far as people's real lives and what happens to them is concerned, there exists a despicable complicity between the globalized logic of capital and French identitarian fanaticism" (Badiou 2003, 8–9). This critique well describes American conservatives, particularly those who emphasize a whitewashed American identity and the need for nonwhites to give up their culture to become provisional sub-Americans. "Keeping up with the Joneses" if you are black, Latino, or Asian American means speaking "standard" English and "acting white."[5]

What all of these visions have in common is that the good life is reserved for a privileged few. All of these visions shut off the possibility of conceptualizing a better world, one in which political, economic, and social arrangements are designed to better the lives of the vast majority of humanity.

Myths Worth Fighting For

The various dystopias described above are all the more powerful because they seem natural, the way that things "just are." Instead, what we must seek to naturalize is the belief that democracy, freedom, justice, egalitarianism, pleasure, health, and human development should be, and will be, consistent with the economic and political systems within which we live and participate.[6] Dystopian visions must be rejected if humanity is to prosper. We must reject what Robert Meister described as the extreme narrowing of our aspirations and visions. Specifically, he argued the twentieth-century quest for "social equality" has been replaced by a vastly narrowed human rights agenda that "is generally more defensive than utopian, standing for the avoidance of evil rather than a vision of the good" (Meister 2011, 2). Otherwise, "if we accept the inevitability of the unbridled capitalist economy and the parliamentary politics that supports it, then we quite simply cannot *see* the other possibilities that are inherent in the situation in which we find ourselves" (Badiou 2010, 64). What we need are new myths that are worth fighting for.

Utopian Possibilities I: Theory

> *Emancipatory politics always consists in making seem possible precisely that which, from within the situation, is declared to be impossible.*
> —ALAIN BADIOU

Of course, whether speculation about desirable alternatives to the way we live now is a plausibly fruitful task depends on one's concept of human nature. If one takes human nature as fixed and immutable, as some of my teachers of political theory in graduate school did, we are condemned to a Hobbesian understanding of humanity in which most utopian solutions are impossible, other than ones that explicitly posit an authoritarian or totalitarian ordering of human life. If one believes with Marx, and for that matter with Fredric Jameson, that human nature itself is constructed, a product of historical circumstance, then there is the possibility of thinking about alternative ways of life that construct different and improved aspects of human nature. One does not, and should not, believe in teleological fantasies about the inevitability of the creation of a new woman or man; one needs only to believe that it is *possible* to envision societies where the basest aspects of human nature as it is currently constructed no longer dominate.

It is easy to understand why thinking about utopias is not in vogue. As Jameson put it:

> The explanation lies in that extraordinary historical dissociation into two distinct worlds which characterizes globalization today. In one of these worlds, the disintegration of the social is so absolute—misery, poverty, unemployment, starvation, squalor, violence and death—that the intricately elaborated social schemes of utopian thinkers become as frivolous as they are irrelevant. In the other unparalleled wealth, computerized production, scientific and medical discoveries unimaginable a century ago as well as an endless variety of commercial and cultural pleasures, seem to have rendered utopian fantasy and speculation as boring and antiquated as pretechnological narratives of space flight. (Jameson 2004, 35)

For Jameson, the hope for utopia is either crushed by the brutality of being placed at the bottom of the global system or rendered irrelevant by the joys of the life lived by the small global elite. Slavoj Žižek made a similar point, but like Badiou, he also highlighted the potency of an ideological component that both makes it difficult to analyze our current dilemmas and promotes false conceptions of utopia:

> Think about the strangeness of today's situation. Thirty, forty years ago we were still debating about what the future would be, communist, fascist, capitalist, whatever. Today nobody even debates this issue. We all silently accept global capitalism

is here to stay. On the other hand, we are obsessed with cosmic catastrophe, the whole life on earth disintegrating because of some virus, because of an asteroid hitting the earth, and so on. So the paradox is that it is much easier to imagine the end of all life on earth than a much more modest radical change in capitalism. Which means that we should reinvent utopia but in what sense? There are two false meanings of utopia. One is this old notion of imagining an ideal society which we know will never be realized. The other is the capitalist utopia in the sense of new and now perverse desires that you are not only allowed but even solicited to realize. The true utopia is when the situation is so without issue, without a way to resolve it within the coordinates of the possible that out of the pure urge of survival, you have to invent a new space. Utopia is not a kind of a free imagination. Utopia is a matter of innermost urgency. You are forced to imagine it as the only way out. And this is what we need today. (Žižek 2005)

The great chronicler of twentieth-century African American life Walter Mosley, echoing Žižek (or maybe it is the other way around?), bitingly explained why utopian exercises are not an indulgence but a necessity: "I want to look into the voracious maw of capitalism to see if there is a way to survive the onslaught" (Mosley 2000, 16). Jameson concurred, explaining that the very task of imagining alternative ways of life, alternative societies, and alternative political, economic, and social arrangements necessitates utopian thinking, despite how weak and out of vogue such deliberations may currently be. Utopian imaginings also allow us to critique the alternatives—a utopia is built to critique "its opposite number" (Jameson 2004, 50). We should think of utopias as open-ended in order to help us imagine alternative futures—but not ones predestined by either the march of history or the triumph of neoliberalism.

The great service Obama did for both black people and a broader set of Americans is that he helped people once again think about the impossible. We should encourage people to retain the Obama campaign's slogan, "Yes we can," even if "no he won't." If we can think about different worlds, perhaps it is not too outrageous to imagine a woman of color seeking the highest office in the land. What other dreams that have been ruled out are in fact possible? If we can think about relatively small dreams of achievement, maybe we can also have larger dreams that imagine a just and democratic reordering in which society and state meet their obligations to all of their emancipated and flourishing citizens. Marta Harnecker explains our task by arguing, "The art of politics is also knowing how to discern which of the impossible things are transcendental impossibilities, and which can be made possible if the necessary conditions are created. In this sense, 'utopia becomes a source of inspiration for political realism, a reference for judgment, a reflection on meaning'" (Harnecker 2007, 70, quoting Adolfo Sánchez Vásquez).

Utopian Possibilities II: Alternatives

At the beginning of this book I invoked David Scott's rejection of the romantic narrative of black politics—a narrative tied to a period in which international black victories ranged from the independence of African and Caribbean nations to the dismantling of Jim Crow in America. Today we are mired in an era of epic tragedy, Scott wrote, in which dreams of independence morphed into the terror of today's failed states and what Cornel West called the "black nihilism" that permeates America's disintegrating black ghettos today. If Scott is right—and there are elements of my analysis of the effects of neoliberalism on black politics in the United States that resonate with his narrative—then what is the basis for utopian thinking?

When we start the process of imagining new worlds, "we must tell no lies, claim no easy victories," as Amilcar Cabral succinctly put it (quoted in Dawson 2011, xii). We must understand the conditions from which we must build. Even though much of modern public policy appears raceless, the black community is under severe attack as a result of the neoliberal political agenda. The Tea Party's devastating attack on public sector unions is, for example, greatly increasing the amount of poverty and misery in American black communities. Steven Pitts demonstrated that public sector employment remains the foundation for black employment that it has been since before World War II. Consequently, an attack on public sector employment is an attack on the black community: "The public sector is the largest employer of Black workers; there is a greater likelihood that a Black Worker will be employed by in the public sector compared to a non-Black worker; wages earned by blacks in that industry are higher than those earned by Blacks in other sectors; and inequality within an industry is less in the public sector compared to other industries" (Pitts 2011, 6).

Workers of all races and ethnicities are facing hard times during yet another jobless "recovery," and building political unity among them is still a daunting task. Lani Guinier (2004) argued that the burdens of integration were distributed unfairly among the poor and working people of the country, thus further undermining the basis for bringing those at the bottom together across racial lines. Building interracial unity was always more difficult than liberals (and in particular white leftists) imagined it would be, since white workers had an investment in whiteness that often led them to privilege race over class when making decisions about political alliances. Any new rebuilding of interracial unity has to confront how to change the white working class's (and, to the degree possible, the white middle class's) perceptions so that they see it as in their interest to ally with nonwhite Americans.

These are just two examples of the very large obstacles that must be overcome by any utopian project. We need a *pragmatic* utopianism—one that starts where we are, but imagines where we want to be. Pragmatic utopianism is not new to black radicalism. King's work, and that of the civil rights movement more generally, was based on the utopian imagining of a much different America—one they were repeatedly told was impossible to obtain—combined with the hardheaded political realism that generated the strategies and tactics necessary to achieve their goals. Indeed, it was the combination of utopian imagining of a better world and political realism that led King to Memphis in support of black sanitation workers. The Memphis campaign, and even more so the Poor People's Campaign that he was about to launch, was designed to explicitly take on what Mosley called the "voracious maw of capitalism" in order to achieve economic justice for all, and in the process build the interracial unity that Guinier correctly observed has been difficult to achieve.

Dreams of a New Society?

I am no longer twenty, so I no longer know everything about how the world should be. I myself do not have anywhere near a developed utopian vision. What I do have are a few tentative suggestions about what I see as necessary to get the discussion started.

My suggestions are not listed in order of priority, and this list is not exhaustive. As Mosley notes, we must all develop our own lists, share them, and argue in public about them.

1. Barbara Ehrenreich's and Dedrick Muhammad's work on the racial realities of the economic crisis and white racial resentment reinforce the need for a conversation on the left about how to openly discuss race in such a way that Americans have to both confront the facts of race in this country and listen to each other so that they begin to understand their real interests.[7] Otherwise white resentment will continue to be aimed at the wrong people (different types of white resentment have different targets). We will have to counter Fox News and its allies. We still have Glenn Beck shouting to a very large and receptive audience that universal programs such as health care are actually "stealth reparations" because they disproportionately affect people of color.

Why can we not have a truth and reconciliation discussion here? In South Africa, truth telling was transformative of both society and individuals. Progressive change necessitates a psychological transformation as well as a societal one. While Meister argues that in South Africa the Truth and Reconciliation Commission became a substitute for success—it symbolized satisfaction with the democratic victory rather than full economic emancipation and full defeat of settler colonialism—he points out that if one looks to Gandhi, then one realizes that reconciliation, relentless political struggle for justice, and eventual victory need not be incompatible (Meister 2011, esp. 51–52). Dialogue and eventual reconciliation would be steps along the way the road to full victory, not full victory itself.

Political theorist Wendy Brown was skeptical of claims of reparations, apologies, and calls for remembrance and reconciliation, basing her point of view on a critique of identity politics very different from the one found in Rorty, Gitlin, and Brubaker and Cooper. Brown argued that identity politics is a form of politics based on weakness and thus has limited possibilities for generating progressive change. Its investment in the past and in suffering all but forecloses the chance that such a movement could become the basis for a democratic future:

> What are the particular constituents—specific to our time yet roughly generic for a diverse spectrum of identities—of identity's desire for recognition that seem often to breed a politics of recrimination and rancor, of culturally dispersed paralysis and suffering, a tendency to reproach power rather than aspire to it, to disdain freedom rather than practice it? In short, where do the historically and culturally specific elements of politicized identity's investments in itself, and especially in its own history of suffering come into conflict with the need to give up these investments, to engage in something of a Nietzschean "forgetting" of this history, in the pursuit of an emancipatory democratic project? (Brown 1995, 55)

She added that "politicized identity" leads to, as Nietzsche predicted, "impotence . . . incapacity, powerlessness, and rejection." Identity, according to this view, becomes a substitute for action, though Brown agreed that these characteristics do *not* describe the civil rights movement (Brown 2001). She was skeptical about the current reparations movement, which she saw as based on weakness, rancor, and perhaps a sense of impotence, and she worried, "Once guilt is established and a measure of victimization secured by an apology or by material compensation, is the historical event presumed to be concluded, sealed as past, 'healed,' or brought to 'closure'?" (Brown 2001, 140).

The current reparations movement need not be based on a politics of rancor (although it has generated plenty of rancor on the part of those who feel their privilege and comfort threatened). Redistributive justice and political power are at the center of the demands this movement has advanced, as is the desire for freedom. Reparations are not about the triumph of the weak; rather, they are a demand for a conversation about justice and the way that racial oppression in the past is linked to black disadvantage today and to the continued existence of an unjust racial order. Indeed, the demand for reparations is frequently associated with the demand for self-determination. Self-determination is not about revenge, and definitely not about victimhood. The crux of self-determination—the key demand of the politicized nationalist and leftist wings of the black power movement—was the collective ability to choose the future that has the highest likelihood of being just; depending on one's ideology, this was a future that was often seen to be egalitarian and sometimes nonpatriarchal, one where blacks would be able to govern themselves. This was a politics more consistent with Marx than Nietzsche. The demand for a discussion of reparations, like the best of the truth and reconciliation movements, is an invitation to discuss how to build a system free from domination, racial and otherwise. I partly agree with Brown's argument that

> making a historical event or formation contemporary, making it "an outrage to the present" and thus exploding or reworking both the way in which it has been remembered and the way in which it is positioned in historical consciousness as

"past," is precisely the opposite of bringing that phenomena to "closure" through reparation or apology (our most ubiquitous form of historical political thinking today). The former demands that we redeem the past through a specific and contemporary practice of justice; the latter gazes impotently at the past even as it attempts to establish history a irrelevant to the present or, at best, as a reproachful claim or grievance in the present. (Brown 2001, 171)

We must begin the process of "making a historical event . . . 'an outrage to the present.'" Yet there is no inherent contradiction that prevents a reparations movement or truth and reconciliation movement from taking on this role. There is no inherent reason that such movements need wallow impotently in the past. How reparations and truth and reconciliation movements unfold is a product of the political contestation that takes place within these movements—of the politics that govern their development. I do energetically agree that Brown's critique well describes much of post-black-power-era black politics, a politics that by and large embraces the values and constraints of neoliberalism, including an emaciated understanding of the politically allowable and feasible. A process of truth and reconciliation, as messy and undoubtedly rancorous as it would be, could help us move beyond the current degenerate state of American politics to a politics that is more truly democratic.

2. The black public sphere, what I have called the black counterpublic, must be rebuilt from the bottom up, and quickly. We need to learn from some of the more technologically innovative forces within the progressive movement to use technology as a way to help people in neighborhoods meet and talk face-to-face,

have these smaller groups link to each other's discussion, and give people at the local level an online set of tools to help them organize themselves. The black public sphere has historically been central to the multiple social movements that have emerged out of black civil society, movements that in turn transformed America for the better. The black public sphere, as King and many others have said, has also been the site of trenchant, effective and influential critiques of democracy in America, as well as the instrument through which African Americans have been able, sometimes effectively, to influence political debate within the country as a whole. That is why it must be rebuilt.

3. People do have to hit the streets. Franklin Delano Roosevelt told progressive members of Congress that he agreed with them and they needed to force him to do what they all wanted. The people best following that advice today are right-wing, racist, but strategic fanatics who have already hijacked political discourse and are on the verge of winning a series of policy and political victories that would be truly devastating. I do not understand why broad sections of the liberal and progressive movements still believe that bringing about serious change, let alone the revolution dreamed of by those such as King, is like a dinner party. It is not. Making change entails being willing to fight. This country needs a social democratic movement with teeth, not one that exhibits better manners than those found at most academic dinner parties. We need a *real* grassroots movement, not the ersatz one foisted on us by the 2008 Obama presidential campaign, as Berlant incisively argues—one that transforms, not just tweaks, the system (2011, 237). If, as Berlant suggested, "the beast of civil society stirs from [a] long sleep," then it is black radicals' task to once again organize so that the beast awakes—once again shaking the

pillars of heaven (2011, 238). It is past time—Albo and his colleagues were absolutely correct when they bluntly reminded us, "The [financial] crisis has shown . . . neoliberal claims to be ideological rubbish" (Albo, Gindin, and Panitch 2010, 19).

For some, the Occupy movement, which began to spread during 2011 and focused intense political attention on various forms of economic injustice and inequality, potentially represented such a movement, but in many regions it grew largely without organized participation from black radicals.

We saw this process begin in Wisconsin as public workers there and across the nation, along with their supporters, began to massively mobilize against the state's right-wing governor, Scott Walker, and his successful attempts to destroy state workers' unions (which were followed by parallel initiatives in other states). As gratifying as the countermobilizations in Wisconsin and elsewhere were, they were entirely defensive in nature. People have to hit the street offensively, not to try to gain back what has been taken away (although that too) but to make demands for action that will improve people's lives, not just barely maintain them at a desperate level of survival.

We must heed Marta Harnecker when she argues, "it is a huge mistake to try to lead grassroots movements by ordering them around, by coming to them with already-worked-out plans" (2007, 78). As she continued to explain, progressives must involve everyone at some level. We need to work to ensure that people can participate at the level they are able, while finding venues through which as many as possible have a stake in progressive social movements.

4. We have to renew our commitment to the value of meaningful work that can actually support oneself and one's loved ones,

and to education for all that not only makes it possible to acquire meaningful and rewarding work but allows each person to discover for themselves what it means to flourish while contributing to society. Berlant put it well:

> Optimism for the present would require the Left to focus on rethinking the structure of labor or work in relation to being-with. . . . There is so little work now, the *sense* of value might as well be reinvented. There is so little commitment to public education now, its purposes might as well be reimagined from the bottom up—but not its people, for education *has* to be the ground for the popular. Not the education that preunderstands a vocation, but education as the inculcated relation to work whose value is not just ends-oriented apprenticeship or putting in time but diffused, risky, and a bit random not just about tasks but about making worlds. (Berlant 2011, 240–241)

5. One area that desperately needs the type of innovation and experimentation generated by pragmatic utopian thinking is the institutional arrangements that govern the functioning of modern civil society, the state, and the relationship between the two. In his book *Democracy Realized*, Roberto Unger argued that to achieve truly democratic societies we must concentrate on institutional innovations and experimentation that put into place a robust and humane democracy. For this type of innovation to be designed and implemented, Unger suggested, a "transformative and solidaristic" political project is necessary. That transformative political process in turn requires that "we speak in the two languages of interest calculation and political prophecy," what I have called the language of pragmatic utopianism (Unger 1998, 12).

One might disagree with Unger's specific institutional proposals, but he was right in stating that institutions shape our perceptions of our interests as well as our ideological predispositions, and that when designing institutions we must remain flexible so as to be able to adapt to new situations, adopt good ideas from elsewhere, and correct mistakes. In short, given the central role that institutions play in shaping our lives, economics, and politics, we can no longer allow them to become rigid and inflexible, unable to serve the needs of society's citizens. Not only must the institutions themselves remain flexible, but we must be willing to constantly innovate, to tinker, to experiment. Only through this type of flexibility and willingness to experiment will it be possible to discover the type of educational institutions Berlant described. Badiou characterized this process as "combining intellectual constructs, which are always global and universal, with experiments of fragments of truth, which are local and singular, yet universally transmittable" (Badiou 2010, 260).

6. We must also reclaim the proud black radical anti-imperialist tradition that began in the nineteenth century and has continued into the twenty-first century. As I have shown in other work, grassroots African Americans generally continue to be against the use of the American military abroad. Further, blacks, unlike a majority of whites in the first years of the twenty-first century, also believed that protesting what one thought was an unjust war was perfectly patriotic.[8] Yet now, for the first time in over a century, black elites are often silent when it comes to commenting on U.S. involvement in foreign wars, particularly those in the Middle East. An anti-imperialist analysis of the mass protest from the streets of Egypt and Tunisia to those of an increasingly leftist Latin America is also conspicuously missing from the black public

sphere. One of the central reasons for quickly rebuilding a strong black counterpublic is to enable the type of foreign policy debates that have been missing from black discourse for much of the last dozen years. We should learn from the moral and analytical failures of the first two periods of black leftist insurgency and eschew *any* blind faith in foreign models. We have to engage in the hard task of trying to understand the currents at work in this world and embrace those that are most promising for increasing democracy and the well-being of humanity, even if they are in opposition to current American foreign policy.

7. Finally, we have to become comfortable with trying to effect change without knowing all the answers in advance. This is the only possible route to the dismantling of oppressive hierarchies of power such as those based on gender, class, and race and their protean intersections. Traditional Marxism is like game theory—both are based on precise analysis of the world but have built into those analyses assumptions that make analysis tractable. Both ultimately recoil from and then ignore the inherent messiness of mass human behavior and politics. In the end our teleologies are shackles. We should not fly blind, but we no longer can afford the certainty that has proved to be a deadly illusion.

Marx despised utopian thinking, but I argue that since we can no longer pretend the social world works in a Newtonian manner, with deterministic laws and a predestined end, we *must* utilize utopian thinking. We can still be realists, pragmatists if we must, but at least we must not limit ourselves in imagining what could be better futures. We can argue about what these would entail and how they could be realized. But dream we must. Those dreams must be debated and eventually transformed into political programs aimed at transformative change.

Where Do We Go from Here?

Pragmatic utopianism demands not just the critically important step of beginning to imagine a just and good society but *action*. Movements must be organized to build that society, test competing visions, and fight off the forces of reaction and privilege that profit from the degradation of the great majority of humanity and the very earth itself. King understood that the answer to his question "Where do we go from here?" demanded a program of action. It demanded mobilization and education. It demanded that black radicals of all stripes—feminist, social democratic, Marxist, and nationalist—step "once more unto the breach, dear friends, once more."

When it comes to the struggle for a just society, for a good life for the majority of humanity, for the end of an ever-mutating but oppressive racial order, stepping unto the breach necessitates that the lessons of the two key periods of twentieth-century black radicalism and the lessons of the sundering be applied and adapted for this century. Independent radical organizations dedicated to fighting for justice and equality for blacks, for an end to the deadly racial order, must be rebuilt. Organizations of black leftists, feminists, egalitarian liberals, and nationalists must be rebuilt or strengthened to take on the issues of economic inequality, the continuing disadvantage that faces blacks and especially black children, gender disadvantage, and the incarceration state. They must stand with the majority of humanity and against the new imperialist land grabs and division of the world by this era's great powers. These powerful forces are no less interested in dominating markets, extracting natural resources (including energy and increasingly food resources), and exploiting cheap overseas labor than the imperialists that black radicals fought in the past. Organizations of black radicals must once again embrace a radical domestic agenda that is tied to a worldview that demands justice for all of humanity, not just those who live in rich and privileged countries. These organizations need to hold elected officials, corporate executives, public intellectuals, and scholars accountable to the communities they purport to represent, exploit, speak for, and study.

The black radical organizations I describe here do bear some similarities to the third-path organizations discussed in the previous chapters. There must be some changes in addition to the ones already specified. First, black radical organizations need to be nimble, innovative, willing to experiment, and flexible—traits often missing from the organizations that have attracted black radicals in the past. Being nimble and innovative means being willing to change organizational forms as needed, even being open to experimenting with different forms simultaneously. This means that there will be a mix of small collectives, medium-sized organizations, and perhaps some of regional scope. There will be black radical organizations, and multiracial organizations to which black radicals belong; some black radicals may belong to both types. These organizations are also more likely to be able to respond to and use the vast amount of information that is the hallmark of the digital age. Large, rigidly structured organization in fields of endeavor from business to government have failed due to their inability to work with and within the ever-growing infosphere. The black public sphere, which we must strengthen and rebuild, already exists partially in cyberspace.

Black radical organizations also need to be far less hierarchical than in the past. This will help them avoid penetration by hostile forces and attempts to silence a small and easily identifiable leadership. But it will also help them avoid a pitfall for black radical organizations of both past periods: being far too undemocratic. We must move from the patriarchal and antidemocratic leadership of past black radical organizations and adopt styles and principles of leadership from the black feminist wing of black radicalism.

Black organizations of different types must once again be willing to test their ideas in theory and practice against those of other forces, but unlike in the past—unless we want to relive the sundering before we have even rebuilt the movement—we must also learn to work with each other despite our differences. Black movements are at their strongest when several different types of organizations with multiple points of views are working within black communities. The united fronts of the past, both the black and multiracial varieties, are desperately needed to confront a system of inequality that viciously attacks democratic movements wherever they appear.

And we must do this now. We must remember one of the positive lessons that black Maoist movements understood a generation ago: "[Maoism] challenged the idea that the march to socialism must take place in stages or that one must wait patiently for the proper objective conditions to move ahead" (Kelley and Esch 1999, 39). Crisis after crisis is devastating peoples and nations; the environment and entire economies are held hostage so that the bankers of the most powerful countries can continue to derive extraordinary profits while gaming the system so that there exists nothing like either a free market or a level playing field. Black radical movements are once again needed to take their place in the growing worldwide struggles against multiple forms of radical inequality and injustice. The example of Hubert Harrison and all of his black radical comrades with all of their human flaws should inspire us to build movements that can in the twenty-first century fight racism, class oppression, patriarchy, and homophobia. We may no longer take the classic third path, but it still has much to teach us.

Conclusion: The Future

"What is to be done?" is the classic question that confronts every generation that believes injustice must be eliminated. As Mosley noted, "creation is the hardest trick of all" (Mosley 2000, 114), but it is a trick we must learn if this nation is to live up to its potential and promise. Another difficult trick we must master if we are to move forward involves "unlearning attachments to regimes of injustice" (Berlant 2007, 296). In order to create we must detach ourselves from the "normal"; in order to determine what is to be done we must forge concrete political programs and be willing to fail, pick ourselves up, adapt, and try again.

If we are not brave enough to face failure, both Cornel West and Alain Badiou reminded us, the alternative is nihilism. Badiou stated it bluntly: "For a politics of emancipation, the enemy that is to be feared most is not repression at the hands of the established order. It is the interiority of nihilism, and the unbounded cruelty that can come with emptiness" (Badiou 2010, 32). Describing the bitter fruit that comes from nihilism in the black community, West wrote, "Nihilism is . . . the lived experience of coping with a life of horrifying meaninglessness, hopelessness, and (most important) lovelessness. The frightening result is a numbing detachment from others and a self-destructive disposition toward the world" (West 2001, 14–15). To climb out of the abyss of

nihilism into which many of our communities have been sink-
ing, we have to remember that "any failure is a lesson," a lesson that
when learned allows us to more strongly move forward (Badiou
2010, 39).

We are too scared to hope, to think big; we are too traumatized
by failures of movements, historical epochs, generations, society,
and government. The trauma of our own failures prevents us
from replacing the waking nightmares of life in this era with
dreams of a better future. We are too traumatized to imagine a
truly *good* society.

As authors ranging from Mosley to Berlant have described, in
a society as deeply conflicted, polarized (particularly racially),
and dysfunctional as ours, collective amnesia and individual
blindness have become the narcotics of choice. It is too difficult
to imagine the crimes that we have committed and continue to
commit as a country; it is too easy to turn a blind eye toward the
evidence before our eyes of daily inequities and failures, whether
it is homelessness, yet another report of a hate crime aimed at a
synagogue or an immigrant or an elderly black or Asian fisher-
man, or the inability of a woman to safely walk down a street by
herself. Our ability to empathize, let alone see how our own interests may be connected to those of the victims, has been severely undermined by the bread provided to the decreasing few
who are well-off and the various forms of circuses available to all
but the most destitute among us.

It is past time to get over it.

The civil rights movement was unique. It was a radical, militant, liberal mass movement. It accomplished great things, it was
responsible for the dismantling of a horrid system of oppression—
Jim Crow, or American apartheid. Are liberals willing to step up

again, to finish the job of winning racial justice, and to take on the even harder task of obtaining economic justice and constructing a humane civil society? Or will it fall again to black radicals (whether feminists, nationalists, or leftists) to carry the load of organizing, as they have not done in some cases for a generation? Will black radicals of all descriptions once again be in the vanguard of independent black movements strong enough to carry us up the mountain that King described in Memphis so many years ago? Are either liberals or black radicals capable of completing the job so that we are no longer stuck halfway up that mountain?

It is time for all of us to step up. As philosopher and liberation theologist Enrique Dussel explained, bringing about change takes character and a willingness to at least consider violating the norms of the time and society within which one lives: "The question of an ethics *of liberation* . . . is that of how to be 'good' . . . not in Egypt or in the monarchy under David, but in the journey of transition from an 'old' order to the 'new' order which is *not-yet* in force. The heroes and the saints do not guide their conduct by the 'current' norms" (Dussel 2003, 140). Reinventing the desire for politics— the desire to stand together—is critical. No movement in the history of black politics better reinvented politics and generated solidarity than the civil rights movement. But another great lesson of the civil rights movement is that ultimately progressive politics is about change—a deep commitment that the world *must* change, and that we must be the ones to change it. Perhaps that is why anarchist movements have never taken hold in African American politics. Or maybe we have been too conventional, too confined to traditional modernist ways of seeing the world. We shall see. In any case, I am deeply convinced that any new politics must remain dedicated to changing the world even while recognizing that the fantasy of being reassured, of knowing fully toward what ends we march, is forever dead. We must rekindle the joy of engaging in politics and bring it together with our centuries-long commitment to noisily but productively disagreeing with each other about means and ends, maintained by the faith that we can make a better world even if we cannot fully see it from halfway up the mountain.

References

Notes

Acknowledgments

Index

References

Albo, Greg, Sam Gindin, and Leo Panitch. 2010. *In and Out of Crisis: The Global Financial Meltdown and Left Alternatives*. Oakland: PM Press.

Anderson, Carol. 2003. *Eyes off the Prize: The United Nations and the African Struggle for Human Rights, 1944–1955*. New York: Cambridge University Press.

Arnesen, Eric. 1994. "'Like Banquo's Ghost, It Will Not Down': The Race Question and the American Railroad Brotherhoods, 1889–1920." *American Historical Review* 99:1601–1633.

———. 2012. "Civil Rights and the Cold War at Home: Postwar Activism, Anticommunism, and the Decline of the Left." *American Communist History* 11:5–54.

Badiou, Alain. 2001. *Ethics: An Essay on the Understanding of Evil*. London: Verso.

———. 2003. *Saint Paul: The Foundation of Universalism*. Stanford: Stanford University Press.

———. 2010. *The Communist Hypothesis*. London: Verso.

Balfour, Lawrie. 2005. "Reparations after Identity Politics." *Political Theory* 33:786–811.

Benhabib, Seyla. 1986. *Critique, Norm and Utopia: A Study of the Foundations of Critical Theory*. New York: Columbia University Press.

Berlant, Lauren. 2007. "Nearly Utopian, Nearly Normal: Post-Fordist Affect in La Promesse and Rosetta." *Public Culture* 19:273–301.

———. 2008. "Cruel Optimism: On Marx, Loss and the Senses." *New Formations* 63:33–51.

———. 2011. *Cruel Optimism*. Durham, NC: Duke University Press.

Biondi, Martha. 2003. *To Stand and Fight: The Struggle for Civil Rights in Postwar New York City*. Cambridge, MA: Harvard University Press.

Boggs, James. 1970. *Racism and the Class Struggle: Further Pages from a Black Worker's Notebook*. New York: Monthly Review Press.

Brown, Wendy. 1995. *States of Injury: Power and Freedom in Late Modernity*. Princeton, NJ: Princeton University Press.

———. 2001. *Politics out of History*. Princeton, NJ: Princeton University Press.

Brubaker, Rogers, and Frederick Cooper. 2000. "Beyond Identity." *Theory and Society* 29:1–47.

Buchanan, Patrick J. 2011. *Suicide of a Superpower: Will America Survive to 2025?* New York: Thomas Dunne Books.

Buhle, Paul. 1991. *Marxism in the United States: Remapping the History of the American Left.* London: Verso.

Button, James W. 1978. *Black Violence: The Political Impact of the 1960s Riots.* Princeton, NJ: Princeton University Press.

Chambers, Simone, and Jeffrey Kopstein. 2001. "Bad Civil Society." *Political Theory* 29:835–867.

Combahee River Collective. 1981. "A Black Feminist Statement." In *This Bridge Called My Back: Writings by Radical Women of Color,* ed. Cherrie Moraga and Gloria Anzaldúa, 210–218. Watertown, MA: Persephone Press.

Cooper, Frederick. 2012. "French Africa, 1947–48: Reform, Violence, and Uncertainty in a Colonial Situation." Unpublished manuscript, paper prepared for the "After 1948: Realignments in Politics and Culture Conference," April 26, 2012, University of Chicago.

Darrity, William, Jr. 1989. "Introduction: The Odyssey of Abram Harris from Howard to Chicago." In *Race, Radicalism, and Reform: Selected Papers of Abram L. Harris,* ed. William Darrity Jr., 1–34. New Brunswick, NJ: Transaction.

Davies, Carole Boyce. 2007. *Left of Karl Marx: The Political Life of Black Communist Claudia Jones.* Durham, NC: Duke University Press.

Dawson, Michael C. 1994. *Behind the Mule: Race and Class in African-American Politics.* Princeton, NJ: Princeton University Press.

———. 2001. *Black Visions: The Roots of Contemporary African-American Political Ideologies.* Chicago: University of Chicago Press.

———. 2011. *Not in Our Lifetimes: The Future of Black Politics.* Chicago: University of Chicago Press.

Debord, Guy. 1995. *The Society of the Spectacle.* New York: Zone Books.

D'Emilio, John. 2003. *Lost Prophet: The Life and Times of Bayard Rustin.* Chicago: University of Chicago Press.

Dirac, Paul. 1947. *The Principles of Quantum Mechanics.* 2nd ed. Oxford: Clarendon Press.

D'Souza, Dinesh. 1995. *The End of Racism: Principles for a Multiracial Society.* New York: Free Press.

———. 2009. "Obama and Post-Racist America." January 28, 2009, http://townhall.com/columnists/dineshdsouza/2009/01/28/obama_and_post-racist_america, accessed December 26, 2012.

Dussel, Enrique. 2003. *Beyond Philosophy: Ethics, History, Marxism, and Liberation Philosophy.* Lanham: Rowman and Littlefield.

Ehrenreich, Barbara. 2008. *Nickel and Dimed: On (Not) Getting By in America.* New York: Holt Paperbacks.

Eley, Geoff. 2007. "Historicizing the Global, Politicizing Capital: Giving the Present a Name." *History Workshop Journal* 61:154–185.

Ferguson, Karen. 2007. "Organizing the Ghetto: The Ford Foundation, CORE, and White Power in the Black Power Era, 1967–1969." *Journal of Urban History* 34:67–100.

Gage, Beverly. 2009. *The Day Wall Street Exploded: A Story of America in Its First Age of Terror.* New York: Oxford University Press.

Georgakas, Dan, and Marvin Surkin. 1998. *Detroit: I Do Mind Dying.* Updated ed. Cambridge, MA: South End Press.

Gilmore, Glenda E. 2008. *Defying Dixie: The Radical Roots of Civil Rights.* New York: W. W. Norton.

Gitlin, Todd. 1994. "From Universality to Difference: Notes on the Fragmentation of the Left." In *Social Theory and the Politics of Identity,* ed. Craig Calhoun, 150–174. Malden, MA: Blackwell.

———. 1995. *The Twilight of Common Dreams: Why America Is Wracked by Culture Wars.* New York: Henry Holt.

Gosse, Van. 2012. "More than Just a Politician: Harold Cruse and the Origins of Black Power." Unpublished manuscript, downloaded from http://www.vangosse.com/scholarly-writing.html, accessed December 26, 2012.

Guinier, Lani. 2004. "From Racial Liberalism to Racial Literacy: *Brown v. Board of Education* and the Interest-Divergence Dilemma." *Journal of American History* 91:92–118.

Guinier, Lani, and Gerald Torres. 2002. *The Miner's Canary: Enlisting Race, Resisting Power, Transforming Democracy.* Cambridge: Harvard University Press.

Gwaltney, John L. 1980. *Drylongso: A Self-Portrait of Black America.* New York: Vintage Books.

Hall, Jacquelyn Dowd. 2005. "The Long Civil Rights Movement and the Political Uses of the Past." *Journal of American History* 91:1233–1263.

Harcourt, Bernard. 2011. *The Illusion of Free Markets: Punishment and the Myth of Natural Order.* Cambridge, MA: Harvard University Press.

Harnecker, Marta. 2007. *Rebuilding the Left*. London: Zed Books.

Harris, Abram L. 1989. "Black Communists in Dixie." In *Race, Radicalism, and Reform: Selected Papers of Abram L. Harris,* ed. William Darrity Jr., 140–147. New Brunswick, NJ: Transaction.

Harris-Lacewell, Melissa. 2004. *Barbershops, Bibles and BET: Everyday Talk and Black Political Thought*. Princeton, NJ: Princeton University Press.

Haywood, Harry. 1978. *Black Bolshevik: Autobiography of an Afro-American Communist*. Chicago: Liberator Press.

Hochschild, Jennifer L. 1981. *What's Fair? American Beliefs about Distributive Justice*. Cambridge, MA: Harvard University Press.

Holt, Thomas C. 2010. *Children of Fire: A History of African Americans*. New York: Hill and Wang.

Horton, Carol A. 2005. *Race and the Making of American Liberalism*. New York: Oxford University Press.

Huntington, Samuel P. 2004. *Who Are We? Challenges to American National Identity*. New York: Simon and Schuster.

Jameson, Fredric. 2004. "The Politics of Utopia." *New Left Review* 25:35–54.

Jefferson, Thomas. 1999. *Notes on the State of Virginia*. Ed. Frank Shuffelton. New York: Penguin Books.

Kazin, Michael. 2011. *American Dreamers: How the Left Changed a Nation*. New York: Alfred A. Knopf.

Kelley, Robin D. G. 2002. *Freedom Dreams: The Black Radical Imagination*. Boston: Beacon Press.

Kelley, Robin D. G., and Betsy Esch. 1999. "Black like Mao: Red China and Black Revolution." *Souls* 1(4):6–41.

Kelly, John. 2012. "Nehru, Bandung, and the Fate of Highland Asia." Unpublished manuscript, paper prepared for the "After 1948: Realignments in Politics and Culture Conference," April 26, 2012, University of Chicago.

King, Martin Luther, Jr. 1957. "SCLC Newsletter." http://eagle1.ameri can.edu/es8783a/mywebsite/beloved.html.

———. 1986a. "A Christmas Sermon on Peace." In *A Testament of Hope: The Essential Writings and Speeches of Martin Luther King, Jr.,* ed. James Melvin Washington, 253. New York: HarperOne.

———. 1986b. "Facing the Challenge of the New Age." In *A Testament of Hope: The Essential Writings and Speeches of Martin Luther King, Jr.,* ed. James Melvin Washington, 135–144. New York: HarperOne.

———. 1986c. "Letter from a Birmingham Jail." In *A Testament of Hope: The Essential Writings and Speeches of Martin Luther King, Jr.*, ed. James Melvin Washington, 289–302. New York: HarperOne.

———. 2000. *The Papers of Martin Luther King, Jr.*, vol. IV: *Symbol of a Movement*. Berkeley: University of California Press.

Laclau, Ernesto. 1990. *New Reflections on the Revolutions of Our Time.* London: Verso.

———. 1996. *Emancipation(s).* London: Verso.

Landry, Bart. 1987. *The New Black Middle Class.* Berkeley: University of California Press.

Lewis, John, and Michael D'Orso. 1998. *Walking with the Wind: A Memoir of the Movement.* New York: Simon and Schuster.

Marable, Manning. 2007. *Race, Reform, and Rebellion: The Second Reconstruction and Beyond in Black America, 1945–2006.* 3rd ed. Jackson: University Press of Mississippi.

———. 2011. *Malcolm X: A Life of Reinvention.* New York: Viking.

Marx, Karl. 1843. "On the Jewish Question." www.marxists.org/archive /marx/works/1844/jewish-question.

———. 1976. *Capital: A Critique of Political Economy.* Vol. 1. London: Penguin Books.

Meister, Robert. 2011. *After Evil: A Politics of Human Rights.* New York: Columbia University Press.

Mendieta, Eduardo. 2003. "Introduction." In *Beyond Philosophy: Ethics, History, Marxism, and Liberation Philosophy,* ed. Eduardo Mendieta, 1–18. Lanham, MD: Rowman and Littlefield.

Mosley, Walter. 2000. *Workin' on the Chain Gang: Shaking off the Dead Hand of History.* New York: Random House.

Palmer, Bryan D. 2000. *Cultures of Darkness: Night Travels in the Histories of Transgression.* New York: Monthly Review Press.

Panitch, Leo, and Sam Gindin. 2012. *The Making of Global Capitalism: The Political Economy of American Empire.* London: Verso.

Parks, Virginia, and Dorian Warren. 2009. "Investment or Invasion? Community Responses to Big-Box Commercial Development in Chicago." Paper presented at "The City Revisited: Community and Community Action in the 21st Century," May 8, 2009, University of Chicago.

Perry, Jeffrey Babcock. 2009. *Hubert Harrison: The Voice of Harlem Radicalism, 1883–1918.* New York: Columbia University Press.

Pettit, Philip. 1997. *Republicanism: A Theory of Government and Freedom.* New York: Oxford University Press.

Pitts, Steve. 2011. "Black Workers and the Public Sector." Center for Labor Research and Education, University of California, Berkeley. http://laborcenter.berkeley.edu/blackworkers/blacks_public_sector11.pdf.

Postone, Moishe. 1993. *Time, Labor, and Social Domination: A Reinterpretation of Marx's Social Theory.* Cambridge: Cambridge University Press.

Ransby, Barbara. 2003. *Ella Baker and the Black Freedom Movement: A Radical Democratic Vision.* Chapel Hill: University of North Carolina Press.

Rogin, Michael. 1990. "'Make My Day!': Spectacle as Amnesia in Imperial Politics." *Representations* 29:99–123.

Rorty, Richard. 1991. "On Ethnocentrism." In *Objectivity, Relativism, and Truth: Philosophical Papers, Volume 1,* ed. Richard Rorty, 203–210. Cambridge: Cambridge University Press.

———. 1998. *Achieving Our Country: Leftist Thought in Twentieth-Century America.* William E. Massey Sr. Lectures in the History of American Civilization. Cambridge, MA: Harvard University Press.

Scott, David. 2004. *Conscripts of Modernity: The Tragedy of Colonial Enlightenment.* Durham, NC: Duke University Press.

Shaw, Nate. 1974. *All God's Dangers: The Life of Nate Shaw,* ed. Theodore Rosengarten. New York: Avon.

Shelby, Tommie. 2002. "Foundations of Black Solidarity: Collective Identity or Collective Oppression?" *Ethics* 112:231–266.

Shklar, Judith N. 1991. *American Citizenship: The Quest for Inclusion.* Tanner Lectures on Human Values. Cambridge, MA: Harvard University Press.

Solomon, Mark. 1997. *The Cry Was Unity: Communists and African Americans, 1917–1936.* Jackson: University Press of Mississippi.

Storch, Randi. 2007. *Red Chicago: American Communism at Its Grassroots, 1928–1935.* Urbana: University of Illinois Press.

Sugrue, Thomas J. 2008. *Sweet Land of Liberty: The Forgotten Struggle for Civil Rights in the North.* New York: Random House.

Unger, Roberto M. 1998. *Democracy Realized: The Progressive Alternative.* London: Verso.

Venkatesh, Sudhir Alladi. 2006. *Off the Books: The Underground Economy of the Urban Poor.* Cambridge, MA: Harvard University Press.

Von Eschen, Penny M. 1997. *Race against Empire: Black Americans and Anticolonialism, 1937–1957.* Ithaca, NY: Cornell University Press.

Wedeen, Lisa. 2008. *Peripheral Visions: Publics, Power, and Performance in Yemen*. Chicago Studies in Practices of Meaning. Chicago: University of Chicago Press.

West, Cornel. 2001. *Race Matters*. Boston: Beacon Press.

Wilder, Gary. 2009. "Untimely Vision: Aimé Césaire, Decolonization, Utopia." *Public Culture* 21(1):101–140.

Wright, Erik Olin. 2010. *Envisioning Real Utopias*. London: Verso.

Wright, Richard. 1956. *The Color Curtain: A Report on the Bandung Conference*. Cleveland, OH: World Pub. Co.

Young, Iris Marion. 1990. *Justice and the Politics of Difference*. Princeton, NJ: Princeton University Press.

Zerilli, Linda G. 1998. "This Universalism Which Is Not One." *Diacretics* 28(2):2–20.

———. 2009. "Toward a Feminist Theory of Judgment." *Signs: Journal of Women in Culture and Society* 34:295–317.

Žižek, Slavoj. *Žižek!* DVD. Directed by Astra Taylor. Zeitgeist Films, 2005.

Notes

1. Foundational Myths

1. Garveyites were members or supporters of the Universal Negro Improvement Association, the organization established by Marcus Garvey, who was the dominant and most powerful black nationalist of the early twentieth century.

In *Black Visions* (Dawson 2001) I argued that two key conceptual foundations of black nationalism within the United States were the belief on the part of most black nationalists that blacks constituted a nation and that race was the fundamental analytical category for understanding African Americans' situation within the United States. While ideologically and historically black nationalism has been an analytical category with shifting and contested boundaries, these two concepts have usually provided the guiding principles for a wide range of black nationalisms.

The historiography of black radicalism has usually included both black leftists and the more political black nationalists. In the early 1970s black feminists also became a core force within black radicalism. Although black feminists were active in black movements at least as early as the nineteenth century, it was not until the 1970s that they became an organized force fighting for black liberation against misogyny and patriarchy. As we will see in Chapter 3, this categorization of black radicalism rejects the view of the CPUSA of the 1950s and 1960s, which labeled all forms of black nationalisms as reactionary. For a fuller discussion of black nationalism within the United States, especially as contrasted to other black political ideologies, see Chapters 2 and 3 of *Black Visions*.

2. While Jim Crow can be said to have formally ended by 1965, with the passages of the 1964 Civil Rights Act and the 1965 Voting Rights Act, there was still active resistance in the Deep South to the provisions of both laws. As late as 1979 there were still demonstrations being organized in Mississippi, for example, which brought thousands of people from around the country to march against continued black subjugation.

The worst effects of Jim Crow would linger for years in many places despite the formal abolition of state mandates.

3. The question asked of respondents was "Do you approve or disapprove of the United States taking direct military action to remove Saddam Hussein from power in Iraq?" In all three years a majority of blacks disapproved of the use of direct military action in Iraq.

4. Here I am using the term *liberal* in its philosophical sense, not necessarily in the ideological sense. I am well aware that there are many for whom neither image of the United States is particularly attractive and who would prefer a polity in which religious differences and other forms of difference are not merely "tolerated."

5. As we shall see in the next chapter, there are several exceptions to this generalization, particularly works within the fields of black and (more recently) civil rights movement studies.

6. The Haymarket riot occurred in Chicago in 1886. It led to the unjust execution of four activists.

7. A welcome major new exception is Michael Kazin's *American Dreamers* (2011), in which black radicalism is treated as a central and critical element of American radicalism. However, the book does tend to somewhat underestimate the radical potential of progressive strains of black nationalism and is too silent on the influence that black radicalism had on the New Communist movement of the 1970s.

8. *Self-determination,* as the term was used by leftists and liberals across many continents during the twentieth century, has many definitions. In the definition most embraced by black activists during that century, blacks had the right to determine their political relation to the United States. Thus it was not a demand per se for secession, although secession was not ruled out as an option. Most black leftists who supported the right to self-determination, however, opposed secession for a variety of reasons both ideological and pragmatic. The attitude toward secession was a major difference between black leftists and many black nationalists.

2. Power to the People?

1. Richard J. Daley was the father of the recent Chicago mayor Richard M. Daley.

2. By "white civil society" I am denoting in particular the racially exclusive associations that fought to maintain white supremacy and its associated benefits of white privilege. These organizations, found in all regions during most of the twentieth century, included white citizens'

councils, neighborhood associations dedicated to maintaining residential and school segregation, and many business associations. Although it is questionable whether the last of these are strictly part of civil society, they closely coordinated their efforts with civil society associations to maintain white supremacy in the social, political, and economic spheres. The Ku Klux Klan and similar groups also would have to be included under this rubric (Biondi 2003; Chambers and Kopstein 2001; Davies 2007; Gilmore 2008).

3. LGBT stands for lesbian, gay, bisexual, and transgender.

4. The category "liberal," into which King is usually placed, denotes in this context the African American ideology of radical egalitarianism; Malcolm X is classified as a "revolutionary nationalist." See Dawson 2001 for an analysis of these and other ideologies found historically within black politics in the U.S.

5. Violence in this context means neither self-defense nor mass spontaneous violence. There has been a long-standing consensus, if not unanimity (with King being the critical exception), that violence used for self-defense was always justifiable if not always prudent. Mass spontaneous violence (as seen in the many urban disorders that continue to this day) generally generates sympathy among black radicals even as it is often recognized that it is counterproductive in multiple ways. Consequently, violence in this context denotes the strategic use of planned violence to achieve political, economic, and social ends.

6. *All God's Dangers* by former Alabama sharecropper activist Nate Shaw (1974) is an excellent account of the rise and fall of black radical sharecropper organizing and the brutal repression it faced.

7. Gilmore 2008, 308. Other examples of important and effective leadership-based black united fronts include the antebellum Negro Convention Movement, which counted among its members such mid-nineteenth-century black luminaries as Frederick Douglass and Henry Highland Garnett, and in the modern era the African Liberation Support Committee, which will be discussed later in this chapter.

8. See Dawson 2001 for a discussion of the ideological and political orientations that differentiate the categories of black liberal and black leftist from each other and from their mainstream American counterparts.

9. They were considered "national movements," as blacks, Chicanos, Hawaiians, and Puerto Ricans were all considered oppressed nations or national minorities by nationalists and many Marxists.

10. For example, see Georgakas and Surkin 1998 for descriptions of the tensions between black and white autoworkers during the late 1960s

and early 1970s as the League of Revolutionary Black Workers took on the forces of racial reaction, including the UAW, in Detroit.

11. See Dawson 2001, particularly Chapter 3, for a discussion of the importance of the concept of "black autonomy to black ideological projects.

12. See Dawson 2011 for public opinion evidence supporting these claims.

13. See Dawson 2011 for an extended discussion of the exclusion of black opinion from the mainstream of American political discourse.

14. The terms "scientific socialism" and "African socialism" developed as some revolutionary nationalists wanted to differentiate the type of socialism practiced by blacks from what they saw as an overly Eurocentric and at times racist Marxist tradition. Further, they argued that particularly by the mid-twentieth century, contributions from China, Indochina, Cuba, and the liberation movements raging at the time in West Africa and southern Africa necessitated a name for the system of thought that acknowledged the broadening of the tradition from its flawed European roots. Often those who practiced what they called "scientific socialism" did incorporate key aspects of Marxist analysis such as dialectical and historical materialism (thus the term *scientific*). Those who practiced "African socialism" claimed that there were indigenous African practices that constituted a different socialist tradition, one no less valid than the European tradition.

15. The lumpen proletariat were a social class that was considered by Marxists to be beneath the working class. They were composed of those people on the margins of society, who had very weak or no ties to the labor force, including the criminal element. Traditional Marxists considered them to be backward and parasitic on the working class. Further, they were considered undisciplined, thuggish, and easily recruited to become police informers. The Panthers rejected this view of the lumpen proletariat, arguing of all groups "the lumpen" had the fewest ties to the system and therefore the least to lose, making them the most revolutionary class in American society. This view was one of the more controversial ones in a program and platform within which traditional Marxists found much to criticize.

16. For an excellent example of this work, see Boggs 1970.

17. The "Combahee River Collective Statement" from 1977 represents a particularly powerful and influential document from the radical wing of the black feminist movement (Combahee River Collective 1981).

18. The Nation of Islam was a partial exception to the trends discussed above. It remained extremely influential well into the 1990s, as indicated by the monumental success of the Million Man March in 1995. Yet the Nation of Islam largely concentrated on nonpolitical initiatives in the economic and civic sphere while mostly eschewing political engagement and mobilization

19. See Dawson 2001, Chapter 1, for a definition of the black counterpublic as an oppositional public sphere.

20. Elsa Rassbach's 1984 film *The Killing Floor* shows the racial conflict that ensued between black and white workers in the stockyards and the problems radical black and white unionists faced when trying to organize there during and after World War I. The film is based on a historical episode.

3. Who and What Killed the Left

1. Following Balfour, it is probably more correct to replace "resentment" in this case with Nietzsche's concept of *ressentiment*. Balfour argues that white men develop *ressentiment* due to the new "constraints on white privilege" that were a result of black gains won through black insurgencies of the 1950s, 1960s, and early 1970s (Balfour 2005, esp. 794–795).

2. I want to thank my colleague Robert Gooding-Williams for suggesting this line of argument.

3. Lawrie Balfour has provided us with several additional theoretical critiques of Brown's argument. One particularly interesting line of argument is when she demonstrates that Brown's critique is applicable to white racial attitudes and behavior. See Balfour 2005.

4. I again thank my colleague Robert Gooding-Williams for suggesting this line of argument.

5. An earlier version of this manuscript had a discussion of the "lost" history of eighteenth- and early nineteenth-century insurrections that featured alliances between various combinations of African slaves, white indentured servants, sailors, and other denizens of what some historians are calling the "revolutionary Atlantic." As the historians note, these alliances and insurgencies were brutally suppressed. I wish to thank Daragh Grant for reminding me of this point.

6. Even a cursory examination of the revolutions of the twentieth century demonstrates the degree to which the concept of the "proletariat" was standing in for a number of other social forces that were different in each national context.

7. I thank Patchen Markell for encouraging this line of argument.

8. The role of Maoism in the black movement of the 1960s and 1970s is masterfully documented in Kelley and Esch 1999.

9. For an analysis that demonstrates exactly this point, see Barbara Ransby's (2003) outstanding biography of Ella Baker and her work both in radical black circles and centrally within the civil rights movement.

4. Modern Myths

1. See Dawson 2011. In addition, see Rogin 1990 for the application of spectacle theory to the United States and Debord 1995 for the original theoretical development of the concept.

2. See Guinier 2004 for a discussion of the phenomenon of viewing racism as, at worst, individual prejudice, a paradigm she labels "racial liberalism." For a powerful if sobering presentation of the deep racial divisions regarding whether racism remains a major force in American society and the prospects for nonwhites achieving racial equality in the United States, see Dawson 2011.

3. Landry (1987) said that much of the black middle class was one paycheck away from disaster.

4. His reference to '68 is to the student and worker uprising in France during May 1968, which threw the country into revolt. It had a transformative effect on French institutions (such as the educational system) and politics.

5. I wish to thank Alice Furumoto for encouraging me to pursue this line of argument. "Acting white" in this context does *not* mean having an education and being middle-class, as it sometimes does in black discourse. As the late Harvard political scientist Samuel Huntington (2004) argued, being accepted as "American" if you were black necessitated becoming white in behavior and cultural practices; he went on to suggest that Latinos in particular, but also those from other civilizations (including what he called "Asian" civilizations), were incapable of assimilating and becoming white. See the prologue in Dawson 2011 for a fuller critique of Huntington's argument.

6. The World Health Organization defines health as "a state of physical, mental and social well-being and not merely the absence of disease or infirmity. The enjoyment of the highest attainable standard of health is one of the fundamental human rights of every human being without distinction of race, religion, political belief, economic or social condition" ("Preamble to the Constitution of the World Health Organization,"

1946, http://www.who.int/governance/eb/who_constitution_en.pdf). The United States is a signatory to the treaty that established the WHO. I thank Alice Furumoto for pointing this out to me.

7. See, for example, Barbara Ehrenreich and Dedrick Muhammad, "The Recession's Racial Divide," *New York Times,* September 12, 2009.

8. See Dawson 2011 for the most recent data on this question. For a broader and more historical discussion of some of these issues, see Dawson 2001.

Acknowledgments

Blacks In and Out of the Left is in many ways the most personal of my works to date. Although the book is not autobiographical, I entered college during the height of the black power era. Even at an elite campus such as the one I attended, one was exposed to the political ideologies of the Black Panther Party, New Left, pacifists, Nation of Islam, pan-Africanism, and black feminism. Given the complexity of the material and times I'm studying, as well as my own peripheral involvement, I have depended even more than usual on colleagues old and new.

Two great institutions have been central in enabling my work on this project. It was the initial invitation from the W. E. B. Du Bois Institute at Harvard to deliver the fall 2009 Du Bois Lectures that provided the initial impetus for the work. The encouragement of its director at every turn, the esteemed Henry Louis Gates Jr., made this work possible in the first place. The gracious hosting by my former colleagues, Gates, Jennifer Hoschschild, Larry Bobo, and William Julius Wilson, and wonderfully engaged critique from them and colleagues such as Evelyn Brooks Higginbotham, Lani Guinier, Tommie Shelby, and Glenda Carpio made the lectures as pleasant and intellectually stimulating as one could hope.

I have been at the University of Chicago for nearly two decades, and a scholar could not ask for a more intellectually challenging and rigorous home. Several institutions on campus have provided venues for testing and refining the arguments in this work. The Center for the Study of Race, Politics, and Culture has provided me with the space to work and critical engagement on all topics related to this work. Center faculty Cathy Cohen, Dwight Hopkins, and Robert Gooding-Williams provided detailed feedback on both the lectures and the resulting manuscript. The political science department has been the site of an intense discussion about the phenomenon of neoliberalism. This discussion has been facilitated by the Department Chair, Bernard Harcourt, who with my colleague Lisa Wedeen both challenged and enhanced my understanding of neoliberalism while also providing a thorough review of the entire manuscript. Political theorists in the department such as Linda Zerilli, Gooding-Williams, and Patchen Markell provided invaluable help in my attempt to sort out the theoretical material in this book. The Chicago Center for Contemporary Theory provided a venue for working out some of the historical material in Chapter 2. Moishe Postone from the Center publicly and privately engaged me in numerous conversations about the political, historical, and theoretical arguments. Lauren Berlant generously engaged in a series of conversations about one of her many areas of expertise, and the section on utopias in particular was much improved as a result. Several graduate students working in this area pushed me hard as always—Daragh Grant, Rohit Goel, Rovana Popoff, and Ashleigh Campi helped me make my work richer and more rigorous.

Many colleagues from around the country helped me work through the arguments I was developing. Phil Thompson, an old friend and valued colleague, was engaged with the material and helped organize events where my work was discussed. In particular I am grateful to the editors of the *Boston Review,* particularly Deb Chasman, for organizing Cambridge-area forums on my work that helped me further refine my arguments.

Extraordinary editorial support was supplied by Lindsay Waters, who exercised great patience with his editorial team at Harvard University Press in seeing this book through to completion. I am sure that he wondered if it would ever be finished. Don Reneau provided a superb editorial intervention by going through the entire manuscript, providing editorial and scholarly feedback at the highest level. The continued shortcomings displayed in this book are entirely my responsibility and are in large part due to my stubbornness in not always following the sage advice of the many colleagues who contributed to this work.

This book is dedicated to the many thousands of activists who attempted to bring true democracy and equality to this country and the world during the 1960s and 1970s. They made great sacrifices to do so, and while there were great accomplishments, much remains to be done. In particular, this book is dedicated to my most treasured comrade, Alice Furumoto, my partner of over forty years, without whose constant support, engagement, and contributions to our work and life together none of this would be possible.

Index

Achieving Our Country: Leftist Thought in Twentieth Century America (Rorty), 128

Acting white, 188, 226n5

AFL-CIO, 83–84, 124

African Blood Brotherhood (ABB), 24, 34; third path of, 37, 38–39; program of, 49–51, 134

African Liberation Support Committee (ALSC), 6, 34, 110–111, 122

African National Congress, 89, 163

African socialism, 105, 224n14

Albo, Greg, 200

All God's Dangers (Shaw), 223n6

American Dreamers (Kazin), 222n7

American Negro Labor Congress, 53–54

Amin, Idi, 163

Anticolonial movement, 59, 63–64, 69, 94–95; on human rights, 75; black radical responses to, 98–100; link with black power movement of, 102–104, 115, 122

Antidiscrimination work, 77–78

Anti-lynching movement, 25, 27, 32, 72

Apartheid. *See* Jim Crow

"An Appeal to the World" petition, 61, 78–79

Arendt, Hannah, 149

Arnesen, Eric, 92–94

Asian American activism, 87, 98–99, 108–109, 141, 170

Assassinations, 41, 71, 97

Atlanta riot of 1906, 23

Atlantic insurgencies, 69, 171–172, 225n5

August 29th Movement, 29–30

Badiou, Alain, 162; on universality, 153–154, 174; on the language of struggle, 184–190, 226n4; on institutional innovation, 202

Baker, Ella, 226n9

Baldwin, James, 142

Balfour, Lawrie, 225n1, 225n3

"The Ballot or the Bullet" speech (Malcolm X), 46

Bandung project, 59, 63–68, 85–86, 89, 94–95

Baraka, Amiri, 165–166

Bauer, Bruno, 146–149

Beck, Glenn, 187, 195

Benhabib, Seyla, 152

Berger, Victor, 26–27

Berlant, Lauren, 208; on neoliberalism, 179, 182; on utopian dreams, 183–184; on public mobilization, 199–200; on education and work, 201, 202

Bethune, Mary McLeod, 75

Biondi, Martha, 80, 83–84

Black arts movement, 165

Black Atlantic movements, 69, 171–172, 225n5

Black autonomy, 90

Black euphoria, 7–10, 186–187, 192–193

Black feminism, 33, 43, 111–112, 221n1, 224n17; on defining "the people," 45–46; on Black Panther sexism, 120–121, 168–169

Black liberalism, 7, 37; Du Bois and, 31–32; on black power, 46–47; civil rights organizations of, 62, 64–65, 124; Double V campaign of, 73–74, 86. *See also* Civil rights movement

Black liberation movement, 60. *See also* Black radicalism

Black middle class, 45, 117–119, 188, 193, 226n3, 226n5

Black nationalism, 6–7, 18, 26, 28, 222n7; of Garveyism, 3, 24, 31–32, 37–38, 221n1; CPUSA's response to, 26, 53, 98–100, 103, 221n1; demands

Black nationalism *(continued)*
    for separate statehood in, 46, 103; black
    power movement and, 87–88, 110–115,
    122; self-determination as separate
    from, 94–95, 103, 115; of Malcolm X,
    102–105; socialist analyses in, 105, 109,
    224n14; demise of, 112–113; concep-
    tual foundations of, 221n1; secession
    demands in, 222n8
Black nihilism, 192–193
Black Panther Party, 4, 34, 36,
    105–107, 115–116, 122; on black
    self-determination, 54, 137, 169;
    state assassinations of, 71; Maoism
    of, 89, 165; *Black Panther* newspaper
    of, 97, 106; organizing approaches of,
    105–106, 224n15; factions, rivalries,
    and demise of, 106–109, 160; sexism
    of, 120–121, 168–169; reform agenda
    of, 129; ten-point program of, 133–134,
    137–142; on capitalism, 136; identity
    politics of, 137–142; labor activism of,
    142; broadening of focus of, 160
Black power movement, 5–7, 37, 96–125;
    Marxism of, 14–15, 18–19, 122–124;
    economic and social impact of, 15–16,
    97; white hostility toward, 18; debates
    on violence in, 31, 223n5; black
    feminism in, 33, 111–112, 120–121,
    221n1, 224n17; third-path organiza-
    tions of, 37–38, 43–44, 48–51, 90–91,
    105–109, 134, 164–165, 169–170,
    205; "power to the people" slogan of,
    45–47; on black self-determination,
    54, 103–104, 137; coalitions of,
    87–88, 99; black nationalism in,
    87–88, 110–115, 122; whitewashing
    of, 96; nonwhite radical organizations
    of, 97–101, 109–112; international
    context of, 99–100, 104–105, 113,
    115, 122; origins of, 101–103; state
    repression of, 106–107, 119–120, 171;
    New Communist affiliations of, 109;
    leadership of, 113; labor organizing
    in, 119; Maoism in, 123, 163–166,
    206–207; identity politics of, 126–152,
    172–173; Rorty's analysis of, 128–134,
    136, 142–144, 149–150, 154; Gitlin's

analysis of, 134–136, 144–150, 154,
    172–173; universalist views of,
    159–161
Black public sphere, 36–37, 114, 121–122,
    198–199
Black radicalism, 7–16, 41–48, 113–125;
    first (communist) era of, 3–4, 41–43,
    45, 48–63, 72–74, 77, 79–81, 84–86,
    115–116, 124; demise of, 7, 37, 106–109,
    112–113, 160–172, 186–187; white-
    washing of, 16–17, 24–25, 33, 39–40,
    43, 222n4, 222n7; debates on violence
    in, 31, 47; self-determination principle
    in, 31, 47, 51, 54, 58, 94–95, 115,
    158–159, 169, 222n8; origins of,
    31–39, 222n8; sexism and misogyny
    in, 32–33, 111–112, 120–121, 168–169;
    West Indians in, 33; public sphere for,
    36–37, 114, 198–199; centrality of race
    in, 44; alternative vision of liberty of,
    47; the sundering in, 47–48, 59–96;
    Marxism of, 48–49, 114–115, 122–124;
    labor organizing of, 53–54, 58–59,
    83–84, 88, 91, 93–94; state violence
    against, 60–62, 71–72, 86, 106–107,
    119–120, 171; moments of potential
    in, 70–71; second (black power) era
    of, 95–116, 124–125, 163–166;
    community-based work of, 115–116;
    electoral work of, 116; Maoism in,
    123, 163–166, 206–207; as sites of
    universalism, 153–161; black arts
    movement in, 165–166; foreign models
    of, 167–168; future possibilities for,
    178, 188–210
Black socialism, 31–32
Black United Front (BUF), 111, 122
Black Visions (Dawson), 9, 141, 221n1
Black Workers Congress, 29–30
Boggs, Grace Lee, 164
Boggs, James, 107, 133–134, 157–160,
    164
Bolin, Jane, 80
Briggs, Cyril, 17, 38–39; CPUSA
    membership of, 24, 51; black
    nationalism of, 49, 53; African
    Blood Brotherhood of, 49–51;
    on self-determination, 51

Brown, Wendy: on identity politics, 129, 136, 145, 196, 225n3; on reparations, 195–198

Brubaker, Rogers, 126, 149–150

Buchanan, Pat, 187–188

Bunche, Ralph, 57, 74, 83, 86

Bundism, 29

Cabral, Amilcar, 167, 193

Capitalism: neoliberal approach to, 7, 92, 112, 178–188; of the U.S., 33, 55, 103–104, 123–124, 156–157, 202–203; Malcolm X on, 103–104, 123–124, 136, 184; Marx on, 123, 178; Black Panther Party on, 136; anticapitalist movements against, 172

Capital (Marx), 123

Carter, Jimmy, 113

Césaire, Aimé, 3, 48, 94–96, 167

Chicago Board of Trade, 182

Chicano activism, 46, 87, 98–99, 141, 170, 223n9

China, 122, 163–170, 224n14; in African liberation movements, 89; Cultural Revolution of, 89, 163; Maoism of, 123, 163–166, 169–170, 206–207

Chinese Communist Party (CCP), 164, 168–169

Citizens Committee for Political Action, 75–76

Civil Rights Act of 1964, 221n2

Civil Rights Congress, 81–82

Civil rights movement, 15–16, 44, 60–61, 69–70, 85, 97, 208–209; as black liberal movement, 31–32, 37, 64–65, 124; Montgomery bus boycott of, 59–60, 63–68, 85–86; organizations of, 62, 64–65; anticommunist purge of, 79–84; whitewashing of, 96; demands and goals of, 99–102; limitations of, 101–102, 176–177; state violence against, 119–120, 171; Gitlin's analysis of, 134–136, 144–150, 154, 172–173; universalist views of, 159–161; Memphis campaign of, 194; Poor People's Campaign of, 194; pragmatism of, 194

Civil society, 114, 121–122. *See also* White supremacy movement

Cleaver, Eldridge, 165

COINTELPRO program, 119, 171

Cold War: state repression during, 59, 60–62, 71–72, 79–86, 106–107; third world Bandung project and, 59, 64–69, 85–86, 89, 94–95; Red Scare of, 71, 76–77, 80, 84–86; McCarthyism of, 84–86, 92, 121–122. *See also* Sundering, the

"Combahee River Collective Statement," 224n17

Comintern/Communist International, 54–55, 58, 89. *See also* Soviet Union

Communist League, 109

Communist Party of the United States (CPUSA), 43–45, 48–59, 114–125; in Depression-era Chicago, 1–3; Scottsboro Boys campaign of, 3, 56–57, 62; loss of black support for, 3–4, 60–61, 72–74, 77, 79–81, 84–86, 99; black membership in, 24, 30, 32, 39, 41, 51, 115–116, 124, 223n6; racism in, 25, 27, 39–40, 52, 57, 58–59, 61, 92–94; on black nationalism, 26, 53, 98–100, 103, 221n1; on revolutionary violence, 31; hegemonic influence of, 45; organizing among blacks by, 52–59, 62–63; National Negro Congress (NNC) alliance with, 57–58; Cold War attacks on, 84–85; on the black power movement, 98; on the civil rights movement, 164

Communist Workers Party, 109

Congress of African People (CAP), 29–30, 105, 109, 165

Congress of Industrial Organizations (CIO), 69, 75–76, 84

Congress of Racial Equality (CORE), 80–81, 102, 112, 113

Connolly, William, 172

Conscripts of Modernity (Scott), 9

Conservatism, 187–188

Cooper, Frederick, 95, 126, 149–150

Council on African Affairs (CAA), 60, 61, 70, 74, 85–86

CPUSA. *See* Communist Party of the United States
Crusader, 36
Cruse, Harold, 39, 90, 164–165

Daley, Richard J., 41
Davies, Carole Boyce, 14, 17–18, 33, 222n4
Davis, Benjamin, 81
Day Wall Street Exploded: A Story of America's First Age of Terror, The (Gage), 19–25
Debs, Eugene, 27, 28
Declaration on Human Rights, 62, 75–76
Democracy, 185–186
Democracy Realized (Unger), 201–202
Democratic Party, 86, 113; alliance with the NAACP of, 78–79, 83; Convention of 1964 of, 101–102; Reagan Democrats of, 127; Southern wing of, 131
De Priest, Oscar, 2
Detroit. *See* Dodge Revolutionary Union Movement (DRUM); League of Revolutionary Black Workers
Dirac, Paul, 68
Dodge Revolutionary Union Movement (DRUM), 4–5, 47, 107
Double V campaign, 73–74, 86
Douglass, Frederick, 91
D'Souza, Dinesh, 175
Du Bois, W. E. B., 24, 31–32, 50, 91; on multiracial radical organizations, 28–31; sexism of, 33; Harrison's critique of, 35–36; on socialist organizations, 40; Cold War suppression of, 61, 80, 81; NAACP work of, 62, 76, 78; Powell's discrediting of, 64; as bridging figure, 69, 74; NAACP's firing of, 79–81, 83; writings of, 81; internationalism of, 115; on universalism, 159
Dussel, Enrique, 149–151, 172, 209
Dystopias, 180–182, 187–188

East Wind, 30
Economic factors: neoliberalism and, 7, 82, 112, 178–188, 193–194; of the

Great Migration, 22–23, 117–119, 225n20; emergence of a black middle class and, 117–119, 193; globalization and, 118, 172–173; of the silent majority, 127, 225n1; impact of the racial order on, 132, 133–134, 156–157; crisis of 2008 and jobless recovery, 187, 193–194; redistributive justice and, 195–198; Occupy movement on, 200. *See also* Labor movement
Ehrenreich, Barbara, 179, 195
Electoral organizing, 116
Eley, Geoff, 25, 84, 149, 172
End of Racism, The (D'Souza), 175
Entanglement, 68–72, 86–88
Environmental movement, 172
Esch, Betsy, 164–166, 168, 169
Ethics of liberation, 149–151, 172, 209
Ethnocentrism. *See* Identity politics

False universalism, 145–152, 172–173
Fanon, Frantz, 167
Farmer-Labor Party convention, 53
Farrakhan, Louis, 143
FBI's COINTELPRO program, 119, 171
Feminism. *See* Black feminism
Ferguson, Karen, 47
Finally Got the News, 6, 107–108
Florida NAACP, 82–83
Foner, Philip, 26, 72
Fort-Whiteman, Lovett, 48
Fox News, 195
Frank, Leo, 22
Frazier, E. Franklin, 57
Freud, Sigmund, 133
Future options. *See* Utopian possibilities

Gage, Beverly, 19–25
Gandhi, Mohandas K., 195
Garvey, Amy Jacques, 111
Garvey, Marcus, 31–32, 36, 81, 123; imprisonment in 1923 of, 37; UNIA of, 37–38; organizing skills of, 38; on black power, 47; on self-determination, 51, 103

Garvey movement, 3, 24, 31–32, 37–38, 52, 221n1; decline of, 45, 54; Back To Africa program of, 49
Gindin, Sam, 156–157, 179, 200
Gitlin, Todd, 127–129, 134–136, 144–150, 154, 171–172
Globalization, 118, 172–173
Gramsci, Antonio, 185
Great Depression, 1
Great Migration, 22–23, 117–119, 225n20
Guinier, Ewart, 80–81
Guinier, Lani, 12, 153, 167, 193–194, 226n2

Haitian revolution, 96
Hall, Jacquelyn Dowd, 44
Hall, Otto, 48, 53
Hampton, Fred, 71
Harcourt, Bernard, 182
Harlem Renaissance, 24
Harnecker, Marta, 162, 192, 200
Harris, Abram, 157
Harris-Lacewell, Melissa, 121
Harrison, Hubert, 17, 19, 34–39, 102–104, 206–207; on multiracial radical organizations, 28–31; on race consciousness, 35–36; Voice of, 36, 38; black nationalism of, 49
Hawaiian activism, 46, 87, 98–99, 223n9
Haymarket riot, 21–22, 222n6
Haywood, Harry, 2, 17, 39, 48–49; CPUSA membership of, 24; black nationalism of, 53, 54–55
Health, 188, 226n6
Holliday, Billie, 133
Holt, Thomas, 118
Hoover, J. Edgar, 144, 171
Housing integration, 77–78
Human rights, 188–189; UN declaration on, 62, 75–76; link with anticolonial struggles of, 75. See also Civil rights movement
Huntington, Samuel, 226n5
Hurricane Katrina, 8, 27, 113

Identity politics, 11–12, 126–145, 172–173; Rorty's analysis of, 128–134,

136, 142–144, 149–150, 154; Brown's analysis of, 129, 136, 145, 195–198; Gitlin's analysis of, 134–136, 144–150, 154, 172–173; of the Black Panther Party, 137–142; contrast to false universalism of, 145–152, 172–173
Industrial violence, 19
Integrated housing, 77–78
Iraq War, 9–10, 92, 222n3
I Wor Kuen, 30

Jackson, James, 85, 98–99
Jackson, Jesse, 87
James, Winston, 33
Jameson, Fredric, 147–149, 189–192
Japan Town Collectives, 30
Jefferson, Thomas, 177–178
Jewish Bund, 29
Jim Crow, 21, 42, 158, 208–209, 221n2; reparations demands for, 6; racial violence of, 20–23, 25, 27, 32, 72, 132–133; disenfranchisement goals of, 23; civil rights movement on, 64, 99–100; Double V campaign against, 73–74, 86; union practices of, 80; Rorty's analysis of, 132–133; formal dismantling of, 176–178. See also Racial violence
Jones, Claudia, 61, 69, 81; on gender and racial exploitation, 14–15, 111; whitewashing of, 17–18, 33

Kazin, Michael, 222n7
Kelley, Robin D., 33, 57, 164–166, 168, 169
Killing Floor, The (Rassbach), 225n20
King, Martin Luther, Jr., 91, 143–144; charges of communism against, 41; assassination of, 41, 97; on black power, 47, 223n4; on Montgomery and Bandung, 65–67; on economic justice, 99–100; on the beloved community, 135–136; on democratic transformation, 162–163, 176–178; FBI campaign against, 171; pragmatism of, 194
Ku Klux Klan, 27, 56, 119–120, 222n2

Labor movement, 88; Dodge Revolutionary Union Movement of, 4–5, 47, 107; League of Revolutionary Black Workers of, 4–6, 105, 107–109, 142; whitewashing of, 16–17; racism in, 26, 27, 77–78, 80, 84, 124, 223n10, 225n20; black participation in, 53–54, 58–59, 83–84, 88, 91, 93–94, 118–119; loss of black support for, 60, 69; voting rights activism in, 75–76; anticommunist purges of, 83–84; demise of, 178–179

Laclau, Ernesto, 149–152, 160, 173

Landry, Bart, 183, 226n3

Latino activism, 98–99, 108–109, 170

League of Revolutionary Black Workers, 115; labor activism of, 4–6, 142, 223n10; as third path organization, 105, 107–109, 134; on capitalism, 136; Maoism of, 164

League of Revolutionary Struggle, 109

Left, the, 19–31, 60; demise of, 11, 161–172, 186–187; racial subordination in, 11–19; whitewashing of, 16–17, 24–25, 33, 39–40, 43, 222n4, 222n7; political violence and, 19–25; antilynching movement of, 25, 27, 32, 72; politics of race in, 25–31, 39–40, 92–94; independent black organizations of, 28–31, 40; origins of black radicalism in, 31–39; "power to the people" slogan in, 46; black-baiting in, 55–56; Cold War repression of, 59, 84–86, 92, 121–122; national movements in, 87–88; on American democracy, 91; economic policies of, 91–92; on U.S. military intervention, 92; Maoism in, 123, 163–166, 206–207; on identity politics, 126–145; Rorty's analysis of, 128–134, 136, 142–144, 149–150, 154; false universalism of, 145–152, 172–173; theory building of, 162–163; reliance on foreign models in, 167–168. See also Black radicalism

Lenin, Vladimir, 123

Leninism, 18, 44, 51, 163

"Letter from a Birmingham Jail" (King), 162–163

Lewis, John, 101

LGBT activism, 46, 223n3

Liberalism, 222n4. See also Black liberalism; Neoliberalism

Liberty League, 32, 34–39, 50, 134

Limbaugh, Rush, 187

Lovestone, Jay, 54

Lumpen proletariat, 105, 224n15

Lynching, 15, 20–23, 72, 133; as terrorism, 21–23; movement against, 25, 27, 32

Machiavelli, 187

Malcolm X, 26, 98, 102–105, 122, 143, 223n4; Organization of Afro-American Unity of, 34, 104; on house and field Negroes, 35; "The Ballot or the Bullet" speech of, 46; on black self-determination, 54, 103–104; on capitalism, 103–104, 123–124, 136, 184; followers of, 104–105; on oppression, 173. See also Black power movement

Maoism, 123, 163–166, 169–170, 206–207

Mao Zedong, 123, 164, 168

Marable, Manning, 81

Marcuse, Herbert, 183

Martin, Trayvon, 96

Martinique, 95–96

Marx, Karl: on capitalism, 123, 178; "On the Jewish Question," 176–177; on civil society, 177–178; on constructions of human nature, 189; on redistributive justice, 197–198; on utopian thought, 203

Marxism, 6, 14–19; male Eurocentricity of, 14, 145–153, 225n6; of black radicalism, 14–15, 18–19, 48–49, 114–115, 122–124; racism in, 27, 169–170; racially- and ethnically-based units in, 29–30; Harrison's critique of, 35; as teleological, 203. See also Communist Party of the United States (CPUSA)

Marxism in the United States (Buhle), 24

Massey Lectures of 1997, 128

McCarthyism, 84–86, 92, 121–122
Meister, Robert, 188–189, 195
Mendieta, Eduardo, 149, 151
Messenger, 36, 38–39
Met Life housing development, 77–78
Million Man March, 44–45, 225n18
Mississippi Freedom Democratic Party
    (MFDP), 100–101
Montgomery bus boycott, 59–60, 63–68,
    85–86
Moon, Henry Lee, 75–76
Moore, Harriet, 82
Moore, Harry T., 82–83
Moore, Richard, 18
Moses, Robert, 77–78
Mosley, Walter, 12, 191, 194, 195,
    207–208
Muhammad, Dedrick, 195
Muhammad, Elijah, 142–143
Muhammad Speaks, 97, 106
Multiracial alliances, 12
Multiracial organizations, 28–31; racially
    and ethnically based units within,
    29–30; blacks in, 31–32, 37, 48–59.
    See also Communist Party of the
    United States (CPUSA)

NAACP (National Association for the
    Advancement of Colored People), 24;
    sexism of, 32; Scottsboro Boys
    campaign of, 56; UN human rights
    petitions of, 61, 76, 78–79; opposition
    to radicalism in, 64–65; board of, 76;
    Democratic Party alliance with, 78–79,
    83; purge of leftists in, 79–84, 86;
    Florida branch of, 82–83; violence
    against, 120
National movements, 46, 87, 223n9.
    See also Black nationalism
National Negro Congress (NNC), 57–58,
    61, 62, 70; CPUSA ties of, 73–74,
    76–77; UN human rights petition
    of, 76
Nation of Islam (NOI), 34, 37, 102,
    225n18; Million Man March of,
    44–45, 225n18; on black self-
    determination, 54; *Muhammad Speaks*

newspaper of, 97, 106; rejection of the
    U.S. by, 142–143
Native American sovereignty move-
    ments, 46, 87
Negro World, 36
Nehru, Jawaharlal, 59, 89
Neoliberalism, 7, 92, 112, 178–188;
    globalized economy of, 118, 172–173;
    dystopian visions of, 183–188
New Communist movement, 6, 87–88,
    124, 162–166, 222n7; organizational
    alliances in, 109; black radicalism of,
    129, 173; Maoism in, 163–166; on
    black liberation, 169–170, 173
New Left, 116–117, 124; whitewashing
    of, 17, 43; on black backwardness, 25;
    Gitlin's analysis of, 128–129, 134–136,
    144–150, 154, 172–173; Black Panther
    influence on, 141; false universalism of,
    145–152. *See also* Black Panther Party
Newton, Huey, 169
Niagara movement, 32
Nietzsche, Friedrich, 196–197, 225n1
Nihilism, 192–193, 207–208
Nixon, Richard, 88, 127, 225n1
Nkrumah, Kwame, 167
Not in Our Lifetimes (Dawson), 16,
    175–176
Nyerere, Julius, 167

Obama, Barack, 8, 175–176, 186–187,
    192, 199
Occupy movement, 200
On Contradiction (Mao Zedong), 123
On Practice (Mao Zedong), 123
"On the Jewish Question" (Marx),
    176–178
Organization of Afro-American Unity,
    34, 104
Ovington, Mary White, 32–33
Owen, Chandler, 24, 30, 31, 39

Padmore, George, 39
Palmer, Bryan, 171
Panitch, Leo, 156–157, 179, 200
Parks, Rosa, 59–60

Particularism. *See* Identity politics
Patterson, William, 81–82
People, the, 44–47
Perry, Jeffrey Babcock, 28, 33
"A Petition to the United Nations on
    Behalf of 13 Million Oppressed Negro
    Citizens of the United States of
    America," 76
Pettit, Philip, 136, 156
Pitts, Steven, 193
Political depression, 186–187
Political race project, 153–154, 174
Political violence, 19–25. *See also* Racial
    violence
Poor People's Campaign, 194
Postone, Moishe, 154–155, 160
Postracial society claims, 175–178
Powell, Adam Clayton, Jr., 64, 67
"Power to the people" slogan, 44–47
Pragmatic utopianism, 194–210
Principles of Quantum Mechanics, The
    (Dirac), 68
Progressive Labor Party (PLP), 169
Public mobilization, 199–200
Public sector employment, 118–119, 193
Puerto Rican activism, 46, 87, 98–99,
    108–109, 141, 170, 223n9

Race riots, 22, 96–97
Racial equality, 7–8
Racial liberalism, 226n2
Racial optimism, 7–10, 186–187,
    192–193
Racial pessimism, 7–11
Racial violence, 19–31; of pogroms of
    1919–1923, 20, 52–54; of Jim Crow,
    20–23, 25, 27, 32, 72, 132–133; of race
    riots, 22, 96–97; against black veterans,
    23, 51–52, 75–76, 77; movement
    struggles against, 25, 27, 32, 72; by the
    state, 60–62, 71–72, 86, 106–107,
    119–120, 171; Florida NAACP's
    response to, 82–83. *See also* Ku Klux
    Klan
Radicalism. *See* Black radicalism; Left,
    the
Rainbow Coalition, 87

Randolph, A. Philip: Socialist Party
    affiliation of, 24, 30, 31–32, 39;
    Harrison's critique of, 35–36; UNIA
    work of, 38; National Negro Congress
    work of, 57–58; on American
    democracy, 72; antifascism of, 73–74;
    suppression of Robeson by, 81; Cold
    War attacks on, 83–84, 86
Rassbach, Elsa, 225n20
Reagan, Ronald, 113
Reagan Democrats, 127
Red Guards, 30
Redistributive justice, 195–198
Red Scare, 71, 76–77, 80, 84–86
Red Summer of 1919, 20
Reparations movement, 6, 137–138,
    195–198
Republican Tea Party, 88, 193, 199
Republic of New Africa, 54, 103, 105
Retort collective, 172
Revolutionary Action Movement
    (RAM), 164–165
Revolutionary Atlantic, 69, 171–172,
    225n5
Revolutionary Communist League
    (RCL), 165–166
Robeson, Paul, 61, 64, 69–70, 80, 81
Roosevelt, Eleanor, 76
Roosevelt, Franklin D., 72, 199
Rorty, Richard, 52, 128–134, 136,
    142–144, 149–150, 154
Rousseau, Jean-Jacques, 187
Russian Social Democratic Labor Party, 29
Rustin, Bayard, 61, 69, 74, 124

Scientific socialism, 105, 109, 224n14
Scott, David, 9, 94, 95–96, 192–193
Scottsboro Boys campaign, 3, 56–57, 62
Segregation, 27, 167–168. *See also* Jim
    Crow; White supremacy movement
Self-determination, 31, 47, 58, 115, 137,
    158–159, 222n8; Garvey on, 51, 103;
    Malcolm X on, 54, 103–104; as
    separate from nationalist projects,
    94–95, 103; link with reparations
    of, 197. *See also* Black nationalism
Senghor, Léopold, 95

Sharecropper organizing, 56, 223n6
Share Croppers' Union, 58–59
Shaw, Nate, 223n6
Shelby, Tommie, 159
Shklar, Judith, 23, 177–178
Silent majority, the, 127, 225n1
Slavery: reparations demands for, 6, 137–138, 195–198; black activism during, 47; master-slave relationship under, 156–157
Social democratic movement, 9, 13–15, 18
Socialist Party, 24, 49, 121; racism in, 13–14, 25–31, 34, 39–40, 44, 50–52; on revolutionary violence, 31
Solomon, Mark, 51
South Africa, 89, 163, 195
Southern Christian Leadership Council (SCLC), 64–65, 101–102, 135–136
Soviet Union: black ties to, 54–55, 88–89, 122; responses to fascism of, 58, 72–74, 89; Operation Barbarossa in, 74; European imperialism of, 93; Stalinism in, 93, 99. See also Comintern/ Communist International
Spanish Civil War, 58, 72
Storch, Randi, 1
Student Nonviolent Coordinating Committee (SNCC), 65, 105, 120, 124
Students for a Democratic Society (SDS), 134, 141, 163
Students Organized for Black Unity (SOBU), 29–30
Stuyvesant Town housing development, 77–78
Sukarno, 59, 63
Sundering, the, 47–48, 59–96; anticolonial movement of, 59, 63–69, 85–86, 89, 94–95; civil rights movement and, 59–60, 63, 64–68, 69, 85–86; state racial violence in, 60–62, 71–72, 86; isolation caused by, 65–68; entanglements of, 68–72, 86–88; bridging figures and organizations of, 69–70, 79–80; voting rights activism of, 75–76; June 1945 meeting and, 75–77; anticommunist purges of, 79–86, 121–122; consequences and lessons from, 86–96; estrangement from white

workers of, 88; loss of international ties from, 88–89; loss of intergenerational continuity from, 89–91, 122
Superposition, 68

Tea Party, 88, 193, 199
Terrorism, 21–23
Third path, 37–38, 43–44, 48–51, 85, 205; classic synthesis in, 50; organizations of, 90–91, 105–109, 164–165; dual approach of, 133–134; doctrinaire turns in, 169–170. See also Black power movement
Thomas, Clarence, 104
Torres, Gerald, 12, 153
Trotter, Monroe, 32, 36
Truman, Harry, 78–79, 83
Twilight of Common Dreams: Why America Is Wracked by Culture Wars, The (Gitlin), 128–129

Underground Economy of the Urban Poor, The (Venkatesh), 179–180
Unger, Roberto, 201–202
United Auto Workers (UAW), 4, 107
United Nations: human rights petitions to, 61, 76, 78–79, 82–83; Declaration on Human Rights of, 62, 75–76; on African American human rights, 83
United Packinghouse Workers, 93–94
United States, 12–13, 222n4; imperialism and capitalism of, 33, 55, 103–104, 123–124, 156–157, 202–203; violence against black radicalism by, 59, 60–62, 71–72, 79–83, 86, 106–107, 119–120, 171; Vietnam War of, 92, 97, 113; economic impact of the racial order on, 132, 133–134, 156–157; intersectional analysis of, 156–157; rise of conservatism in, 167–168, 187–188; monetary system of, 182; penal system of, 182; American dream of, 183–184; Middle East wars of, 202–203. See also Anticolonial movement
Universalism, 145–161; Eurocentric approaches to, 145–153, 172–173; black

Universalism *(continued)*
  movements as sites of, 153–161; need
  for contextualization in, 154–157,
  225n6; broadened conceptions of, 173.
  See also Identity politics
Universal Negro Improvement Association (UNIA), 32, 37–38, 52, 54, 221n1.
  See also Garvey movement
Untermann, Ernest, 26–27
Urban League, 81
Utopian possibilities, 178, 188–210;
  neoliberal versions of, 183–188;
  theoretical consideration of, 189–192;
  obstacles to, 192–194; pragmatic
  approaches to, 194–202; truth and
  reconciliation in, 195; redistributive
  justice and reparations in, 195–198;
  black public sphere in, 198–199; public
  mobilizations in, 199–200; meaningful
  education and work in, 200–201;
  institutional innovations in, 201–202;
  anti-imperialist engagement in,
  202–203; flexibility in, 205–206

Venkatesh, Sudhir, 179–180
Vietnam War, 92, 97, 113
Violence debates, 31, 47, 223n5. *See also*
  Racial violence
Voice, 36, 38
Von Eschen, Penny, 71
Voting Rights of 1965, 221n2

Walker, Scott, 200
Wallace, George, 88, 127
Wallace, Henry, 79
Wall Street bombing of 1920, 19–20
Wayne State University newspaper *South
  End*, 5
"We Charge Genocide" petition, 82–83
Wedeen, Lisa, 185
Welfare bifurcation, 13
Wells, Ida B., 21, 25, 32–33, 36
West, Cornel, 192–193, 207–208

West Indian activists, 33
What Is to Be Done (Lenin), 123
White, Walter, 74, 78–79, 81, 82
White supremacy movement, 42, 77, 94,
  98–99; of white civil society, 42,
  222n2; current expressions of, 96;
  black radicalism's challenge of,
  114–115. *See also* Jim Crow; Racial
  violence
Whitewashing, 16–17, 33, 43, 222n4; of
  1960s and 1970s leftism, 96; of
  American identity, 187–188
Wilder, Gary, 94–96
Wilkins, Roy, 74, 78–79, 83
Wisconsin public worker mobilization,
  200
Women, 32, 46, 168–169; suffrage
  movement of, 25; Liberty League
  of, 32, 34–39; sexism and misogyny
  toward, 32–33, 111–112, 131, 168–169;
  black feminism of, 33, 111–112,
  120–121, 221n1, 224n17; economic
  exploitation of, 156–157
Workers Party, 53
World War I, 23, 51–52, 117
World War II, 73–75; Double V
  campaign of, 73–74, 86; black
  veterans of, 75–76, 77. *See also*
  Sundering, the
Wright, Erik Olin, 155–156, 185
Wright, Richard, 2, 39, 59, 89

X. *See* Malcolm X

Young, Iris, 136, 173
Young Lords Party, 29–30

Zerilli, Linda: on outsidedness, 132, 133;
  on universalism, 146, 148–154, 160,
  173
Zhou Enlai, 59, 89
Žižek, Slavoj, 190–191